MW01170356

Amusing to Profound

MY CONVERSATIONS
WITH ANIMALS

I and II

Suzanne Ward

ISBN 978-0-9717875-5-1

Library of Congress 2009900754

Second Edition 2012

Album photographs by
Bob Chapman, Raquel Fonseca, JC Lampee,
Ani Avedissian and Anita Barry

MATTHEW BOOKS
P.O. Box 1043
Camas, Washington 98607

www.matthewbooks.com
suzy@matthewbooks.com

This book is dedicated to
EARTH'S ANIMAL KINGDOM

Heartfelt thanks to

My husband Bob, for everything you will read about his partnership in our fur family's care;

our granddaughter, Raquel Fonseca, who used her artistry and computer skills to design the book cover;

Julia DeVlieg and Camille Richards, whose suggestions gave this story the fullness and polish it needed;

Ann Miller, whose expertise and caring turned computer files and an assortment of photos into this book; and

all the dear animal souls who have given me such great fulfillment.

Amusing to Profound

MY CONVERSATIONS
WITH ANIMALS

I and II

CONTENTS

I

II

Our Family Album

I

Prologue

"*I love to ride.*" That's what Sparkle said. The Brittany spaniel we adopted had just opened my telepathic communication with animals.

Since that day in 2002, many others in Earth's animal kingdom also have talked with me. Their comments in this book show that the breadth and depth of their intelligence and emotions far exceed what is attributed to them.

Most of my conversations have been with dogs, some of whom have told me what Big Dog, the "canine angel," teaches the puppy souls before they are born and how he guides them once they are here. They have told me about life "there," the way they refer to the spirit world we call Heaven.

Dolphins, squirrels, deer, llamas, birds and a horse, sea lion, lizard and cricket also have talked with me. Like the dogs, some things they have said are astonishing, others are amusing, and all give glimpses into their hearts and minds.

Long before Earth's recorded history, animals and people lived peaceably together and spoke telepathically. In a few short years, that once again will be commonplace in our world.

Preface

Stories and films about animals doing extraordinary things are heartwarming, even astounding. Dolphins, dogs and elephants save people from drowning or other harm, and pets act like smoke alarms and waken their families. Service animals make life infinitely more cheerful, secure and convenient for their human companions, and dogs bring smiles that hasten the recovery of people in hospitals or brighten the days of hospice patients. There are unlikely cross-species friendships, even mothers of one species who nurture infants of another, and wild or domesticated animals remember humans they had not seen for a long time.

The animals in this book haven't done anything out of the ordinary. It is because there is nothing at all remarkable about them that what they talk about is so important—they are typical representatives of their sections of the animal kingdom. True, we can interpret our pets' attitudes and needs through their expressions and behavior, but really, who trains whom to understand those signals? Exactly what dogs or cats or horses or birds or pigs or llamas or dolphins are feeling and thinking lies in the abyss between their hearts and minds and our languages. What animals have told me helps to build a bridge over that chasm.

I don't think of myself as an animal communicator. I have known individuals who are. Their abilities can include hearing a word, or a few words, and intuitively knowing what the animals mean; diagnosing health problems; receiving images of animals' surroundings or symbols with specific interpretations; sensing the family's energy that affects their pets; gleaning insight into animals' past experiences and connecting with those who are deceased; and either remotely or on site, feeling the same emotions and physical discomfort as do their clients that swim, fly, hop, slither, or run about. How I respect these gifted individuals who are godsends to so many animals and their caretakers!

My abilities, although tremendously fulfilling, are much less extensive. I hear the voices of animals I know or am with if they want to talk with me—not all to whom I speak answer me. Sometimes I feel their emotions and I receive images sent by those who have moved on to the spirit world we call Heaven.

Most animals who have talked with me didn't initiate our conversation, but some have spoken first in response to my thoughts. I hear them speaking, but this is not audible to people who may be sitting beside me. Although I hear animals' voices in English because the language is common to them and me, an integral aspect of telepathic communication is a translation system that is similar to different computer software programs that can "talk" to each other.

Animals speak articulately and logically, without tact or flattery or ambiguity, those nuances we acquire to best deal with whatever a situation calls for. Their voices differ in tone and inflection, just as ours do; and their talking styles and topics are reflections of their personalities and interests, just as our conversations are extensions of who we are.

Some animals ask a question or reply to mine in simple, short sentences—that is enough for them—and others carry on a conversation and use phrases to explain things I didn't know before they told me. Occasionally one uses a word that is new to me, like the one little Fruity used when we were walking along the side of the road and his back leg got hung up on a briar stringer. "*What is this?*" I told him it was a briar. "*What is a briar?*" "It's a different kind of grass." "*Well, it has pickies.*"

Many of our dogs' comments, like that one, delight me but are insignificant to them—they just tell it like it is. And there is no fooling animals—they know what we are thinking and feeling as well as what we say to them and to each other. Telepathy is the energetic transfer of thoughts and sensations from one consciousness to another, and the capacity to communicate by this means is innate, a part of the soul of every life form.

Eons ago, civilizations on Earth conversed telepathically with family and friends in spirit life and with animals on the planet. Then, animals lived peaceably among themselves and with the people, and that is the way it always has been in Earth's spirit world. A glorious aspect of the spiritual transformation underway in our world is that in a few years, we will be living in harmony with each other and all of Nature once again, and everyone will be talking naturally with animals.

They have a far wider range of intelligence and emotions than most people attribute to them, and in some respects, the higher species in the animal kingdom are more perceptive than we are. They are much more sensitive to energy than most of us and they know when the spirits of "deceased" people or animals are present. As multidimensional beings, they go back and forth between the physical and the spirit worlds, so they know there is no such thing as death. All the dogs I have talked with refer to Earth as "here" and the spirit world as "there," and after transitioning, they tell me what they are doing "here."

Without the capacity to deceive or betray, animals are honest and loyal and their love for their human families is unconditional. Those who had bonded especially closely with persons may return to them later in the same kind of body or one of a different breed, but with the same unmistakable personality and disposition. Just as human souls evolve through lifetimes of learning through experience, so do animals, and it is not uncommon for human soul energy to incarnate as an animal to experience that kind of life.

An essential part of human soul evolution is the awareness that everything in this universe is energy fluctuating at one frequency or another and that no life is separate from another life in any form—each is a part of God, by whatever name one calls the Supreme Being. The interconnectedness of All is why it is so important that we respect, nurture and honor all life in the animal and plant kingdoms.

How I wish I had kept a journal of everything animals have told me during the past six years! I did make notes of many verbatim comments or wrote them in emails to family and friends, and it is those that I am sharing with you in *Amusing to Profound—My Conversations with Animals.*

Suzanne Ward
January 2009

The Beginning

"I love to ride."

What a curious thing for Bob to say—I was riding, he was driving. Half an hour before we had said goodbye to our dear friend Betsy Jones-Moreland, whose life was dedicated to her Questover Animal Rescue, then we started the two-day trip home with Sparkle, the gentle old Brittany spaniel we had adopted. I looked over at my husband, about to ask why he would make such an odd remark, when I heard *"I'm glad you're taking me home with you."* That would have been totally outlandish coming from him, but he wasn't saying a word.

I glanced in the back seat, where Sparkle was lying as confidently as if she had spent her whole life there. Feeling really foolish, nevertheless I said, "Sparkle, did you just speak to me?" *"Yes. I said I'm glad you're taking me home with you."*

My telepathic connection had opened eight years before, in 1994, with my son Matthew, who was in a fatal vehicle crash in 1980. Soon after our conversations started, he introduced me to many other beings in the spirit world where he was living and in physical civilizations far advanced of our own spiritually, intellectually and technologically. And only a few months prior to this trip, my telepathic communication was further expanded by the Devic and plant kingdoms. Still, it was startling to hear Sparkle's voice, and of course I had no idea what I would be learning from animals after that moment when she so casually but immeasurably widened my world.

Sparkle

Our veterinarian said Sparkle was about six or seven, and it was not due to overeating but years of steroids to treat a chronic skin condition that caused her irremediable obesity. Since I could not undo what had been done, at least I could discontinue it. I gave Sparkle the recommended antihistamine and the same raw food diet that was so healthy-making for our other dogs, and in those respects, she flourished. But despite Bob's and my repeated assurances that she was beautiful, our demure sweet lady was self-conscious about her misshapen body for the seven years she was with us.

Her delicate face was beautiful and so were her soft brown eyes and liver-spotted, snow-white silky fur. Frequently I would mention those lovely features and say, "You are Mommy's beautiful girl." But she would counter with "*I know I'm too fat,*" or "*I want to be thin like other dogs,*" and in one of her periodic check-ups, the scale showed she had lost two pounds. Hearing her doctor and me discussing that, Sparkle asked, "*Did I really lose two pounds?*" I told her, "Yes! Yes, you did!" But lost pounds or not, she felt no difference in her cumbersome body with its doublewide back that looked as if any minute it could crush her stick-thin legs.

I don't know if she understood that she had given my life a wondrous new dimension, but she knew she was special in some way and greatly loved. Sometimes when I said, "I love you, Sparkle—you are my special baby," she would say *"I know, I feel it,"* but more often she just cuddled closer to me.

Never a real conversationalist, she seemed content with loving attention and comments from me, and occasionally she spoke to me first. One day when I stopped to caress her, she asked, *"How did you know what they needed before you could hear them?"* "I had to guess and hope I was right. But you taught me mind-talk, so now I can ask them and they tell me." That was enough for her to know. It was like our other short exchanges that reinforced her special importance to me, and those times she didn't mention her unhappiness about her body.

Like our other dogs, Sparkle enjoyed roaming around our property and going for walks, but when the rest were noisily dashing around in the house, she would quietly lie watching. I'm not certain that she even joined in when the whole gang was outside and started their proprietary "This is *our* street" racket. This woodsy area is secluded and serene, but there is enough activity to keep our fur family on the alert—neighbors walk their dogs by day and coyotes howl at night, the occasional car or delivery truck drives by, and especially the weekly trash pick-up requires a lot of barking to keep us safe.

Sparkle never whimpered during the painful recovery after the difficult removal of two benign cysts, and she was healthy for two years afterwards before her weight made mobility, then breathing, increasingly difficult. It had been quite a while since she had been able to climb into Bob's chair in our bedroom, the place she had chosen right at the start to be her bed. Always when I asked how she was feeling, she would say, "*I'm fine,*" but finally she admitted that she hurt. The years of steroids were exacting their toll, and the only thing the hospital staff could do was give her more potent medication. Each time I gave it to her, I told her it would make her feel better, but if it did, it was only briefly.

It was the middle of the night in February 2008 when she walked into the bedroom after being outdoors—her face was cold and damp as she nuzzled my hand. "*The new medicine isn't working. Please tell my doctor to help me go there and stay.*" I told her that if she felt the same in the morning, her daddy and I would take her. Still sitting by my bed when I wakened a few hours later, she looked up at me and said, "*I feel the same. You said you will take me.*"

She lay quietly on my lap during the ride to the hospital, but once there, she was as frisky as a puppy, sniffing in the back rooms as excitedly as if she were tracking a rabbit or a squirrel. Had I so terribly misunderstood what she told me? But when Monica, our treasured veterinarian, came in, Sparkle lay down and Bob and I sat beside her. She put her head in my lap and looked up at me. "*Thank you, Mommy. Please tell Daddy and my doctor thank you.*"

Monica injected a mild sedative and Sparkle closed her eyes. We all had tears, knowing that in a few minutes, it would be the lethal shot, but seconds later I heard Sparkle shout, "*I'm here! I'm here. They let me come this fast! Look at me!*" and she sent me her image. This beautiful young, slim Brittany spaniel first posed as if she had won Best of Show at Westminster, then ran like the wind to catch up with elephants, giraffes and big cats grazing in the distance.

Monica looked dubious when I repeated what I had just heard, but when she put the stethoscope on Sparkle's chest, there was no heartbeat. Our beloved gentle lady, whose gift had so enriched my life, had been gifted with moving on that swiftly to receive what she had been denied in this lifetime, a body she knew was beautiful.

Scrapper - Summertime

A few months before Sparkle came and expanded our fur family to six, a virulent infection suddenly raged in Summertime and abruptly caused his deafness. It was traumatic for all of us.

By that time he had been with us for over ten years, the first three with the name Scrapper and the rest as Summertime. He also came from Betsy's Questover haven for homeless and injured dogs, cats and other needy animals. That was my destination one summer day in 1991.

The drive from our new home in San Jose to Betsy's, north of Los Angeles, took much less time than I had estimated, and she wasn't there when I arrived with our extra TV set and other things she could use. However, someone else greeted me. Sitting in her driveway was a golden cocker spaniel, his leash wound around a large stone atop a carton with a note: *Please find a good home for Scrapper* and signed Domingo. Of course I felt my meeting this excited fellow of the breed especially dear to my heart was serendipitous—it couldn't have happened if I had been able to go when I expected, and it was convenient for Betsy that I would be coming two days later.

The note was from the man who sometimes helped her with kennel repairs. He gave her the telephone number of the couple who had asked him to find a home for the dog, and when I called, the woman told me about the most recent

15

months in this beautiful dog's life.

Six months previously she and her husband had seen him cowering in a downpour, his neck tied to the rope that bound a tall stack of sodden newspapers. They conjectured that before the rain started, he had been picked up by someone who felt that securing him rather than letting him run loose at least would keep him safe from traffic. To assure that he had no health condition that could affect their cat, they drove directly to the veterinary clinic, where they learned that he was healthy and about two-and-a-half years old.

Certain that his family would be overjoyed to welcome home their wonderful pet, each day after work for the next three weeks they took the dog and looked for his home. They already had covered nearly a quarter-mile radius from the spot where they had found him when they came to a property so litter-ridden and derelict that they didn't want to even enter the yard. But they did, sidestepping trash on their way to the tiny crumbling concrete stoop, and knocked on the door.

It was opened by a man whose undershirt and shorts were as filthy and smelly as the room behind him was disorderly and reeking of foul odors. He glared at them, yelled that he didn't want that goddam thing back and didn't care what they did with it, and he slammed the door.

The woman told me they wouldn't have left Scrapper there anyway. They gave him that name because he and their cat fought in their fenced backyard domain, and it was because of those fracases that six months after they found Scrapper, they felt they had to find him another home. She was glad to know it would be with me and that he would have dog companions, breakfast meat and biscuits, a warm dinner, lots of treats and all necessary medical care.

And so I happily started the drive home with Scrapper sticking his head out the back seat window.

Not only was he not housebroken, but he growled and nipped when food was offered by hand, and he didn't mingle with our other dogs. Regardless, I felt deeply attached to him, certain that with patience and training, he would feel secure and his behavior would improve. After several months with no change at all in his attitude, I felt discouraged—should I find another home for him? So surely it was not by accident that I saw a newspaper article about an animal psychic in a nearby town.

I wondered why this attractive woman looked sad as she held the picture of Scrapper until she started telling me his story. He and his littermates were born in a filthy home and were only a few weeks old when a man started beating their mother with a broom handle because she had taken his sock for her babies to play with. To escape the blows, she ran out the open door, and the puppies heard her screams when she was hit by a passing car and left to die in the street.

The psychic didn't know what became of the other puppies, but the man kept the one we met as Scrapper. Instead of training or taking him outside to urinate and defecate, the man kicked him and shoved his mouth into the messes; and after days without feeding the dog, he taunted him by offering food, then pulling it away. That cruelty lasted about two-and-a-half years, then the man simply dumped him.

The loss of his mother before he was weaned and the brutal treatment that followed had permanently traumatized our dog—he never could be housebroken and might never stop his aggressive behavior. If we could not live with that, the psychic said, please be merciful. Instead of giving him to someone else to treat as they might, spare him that additional trauma and have him euthanized. Both she and I had tears as I assured her that as long as I lived, no one would ever hurt this dog again.

Now, these many years later, he was hurting and frightened by his sudden deafness and I couldn't do a thing to help him. His eyes and his cries begged me to fix whatever fearsome thing wouldn't let him hear me or even his own barking. It was painful to see him during those weeks before he adapted to his silent world and his loneliness within it. I remembered what I had told the animal psychic long ago and afterwards, how often each day I would say, "Scrapper, I'll always love you and take care of you." I thought and spoke about him as touching my very soul.

That hour with the psychic had been a turning point for Scrapper and me. I stopped saying "Ouch!" when his nips cut into my hand as he grabbed the special treats I held out and I never scolded him again about pee puddles and poop piles in the house. Instead, I would tell him "Please trust me, Scrapper—I'll never take your food away," or "It's OK, Scrapper, I know you can't help it." He responded by starting to take treats more gently and sometimes he even kissed me when I picked him up. Even though his nervousness remained, he became much more affectionate with Bob too and started playing with our other three dogs.

By the time we moved to Washington state, two of those dear fur kids had died—only Scrapper and Damian made the trip with us. However, our new home on several wooded acres in a private neighborhood out in the country was ideal for dogs, and five more found their way to us in the next few months. We also were fostering dogs for the little local no-kill Humane Society shelter, and Scrapper was especially on the outs with a male twice his size. The dynamics changed with each addition, and maybe Scrapper needed to show that his place in our family was secure.

It was providential that I heard about Linda Tellington-Jones, well known animal communicator and healer, who was conducting a workshop for families and their pets. I took Scrapper. Linda sensed the deep pain and fear beneath his nervous whimpering and said it might help to change his name from a word that is associated with fighting to something mellow in meaning and sound. "Summertime" leaped into my mind and Scrapper didn't miss a beat in answering to his new name.

And mellow he did. He became the canine world's best kisser, often running up to me so I would lean over and he could reach my cheek. He stopped grousing about Brillo and Cloudy sleeping on the same bed that until they joined the family, only he and Damian had shared with Bob and me. In that respect, it was just as well that dear old Damian's decreasing mobility prevented his jumping up there and he contentedly slept on the floor by my side of the bed. And it is good that Summertime had accepted all the newcomers in our family before his long-time friend Damian went so far downhill that his eyes pleaded for release and Monica came to our home to do that for him.

But going back a long ways, before our move from San Jose to a neighborhood east of Vancouver, Washington, and when Summertime was still called Scrapper—I'll always think of him as my Summertime—he had shown the gentle side of his nature. A white rat found its way through our doggie door. Now and then Bob or I would see it scampering away from the little plate of dog biscuits by the water dishes, but it was almost a month before we discovered that it had set up housekeeping in a hole in the wall behind my office sofa. The same day it entered the trap Bob fashioned, we bought a cage with a wheel and steps leading to platforms, placed it on the kitchen table in front of the triple window, and named its new occupant Molly. Our veterinarian said she was a healthy and apparently happy furry young lady.

Scrapper was enamored of Molly. The most agile dog I have ever seen, he easily made his way onto the kitchen counter, where he ate the tomatoes ripening on the window sill; and into the bathroom washbowl, where he would lie and watch me put on makeup or trim Bob's beard. There was no way I could keep him off Molly's table, and I was relieved that she was not at all bothered by his lying inches away, whining and snuffling his adoration.

When he pawed at her cage, she simply went up to the pegboard room Bob had made so she could have a private space, but before long, she started training Scrapper. When he put a paw on her home, she stood on her haunches and held up her forepaws. If there was any communication other than that, I didn't know it—I just saw Dog quickly adapt to Rat's instructions.

One day right after he had clambered up onto his favorite spot, Molly started chirping and went to her cage door. I walked to the far side of the table and opened it. She jumped out and ran around the cage, stopping a few inches from Scrapper's snout and went into her training stance. He didn't flicker a whisker, just lay there for fifteen minutes or so while he and I watched his little friend playing all around him until she went back into her home and up the steps to nap in her bedroom.

For the two years Molly was with us, her cage was her private space. Her much larger world was behind the closed door of our TV room/office, where she was safe from our other dogs and she could scamper all over the computer keyboard, her special interest, and wherever else she felt like exploring. When Scrapper and Bob or I joined her, she would leave wherever she was to be near her canine admirer, and when she tired of playing around him, she would jump to the bookshelves, yawn a few times and go to sleep.

I never imagined that I could so dearly love a rat, but Molly captured Bob's and my hearts as well as Scrapper's. It was a bleak day when our veterinarian diagnosed Molly's mammary cancer. When the tumors made it difficult for her to pick up food, I handed it to her, but the day came when the compassionate vet told me it was time to hold Molly and say goodbye. It was almost as sad to see Scrapper sit by her cage in the garage, pawing at it and crying; and once it was gone, wander around the house looking for his special little friend.

Those were some of my thoughts about Scrapper-come-Summertime as he was long before his abrupt deafness. Then Sparkle came and suddenly brightened his life with what he called "think-talk" and our other dogs called "mind-talk." Of all our dogs, his conversations with me were the most lengthy and profound. One day he mentioned something that I couldn't imagine he would know, that God is everything and everywhere.

"Summertime, how do you know that?"

"*Big Dog told us.*"

"Is Big Dog what you call God?"

"*NO!* **God** *is God! Big Dog is the mentor and disciplinarian of all dogs.*"

He told me that puppy souls live "there" before they are born, and Big Dog teaches them what they need to know so they can do their jobs well—hunt, herd, guard, track scents, be a sweet little companion—depending on the breed each puppy soul would become. Big Dog teaches them what to expect from people and how to behave and how to fend for themselves if they get lost.

"Summertime, after puppies are born, do they remember everything Big Dog taught them?"

"*They know it as instinct and they remember the lessons when they need to. When dogs go there to visit, Big Dog tells them if they need more instruction and he knows who does. There always are classes because the new puppy souls need them and the ones who visit go to reminder classes if Big Dog tells them to.*"

"I see. It sounds as if Big Dog is very old and wise."

"*He's God's special helper for dogs and he knows every-thing there is to know. He has lived there ever since dogs were made, but he'll never get old.*"

"So he knows God?"

"*Of* course *he does!* Every *dog knows who God is! Don't* you *know?*"

"Yes, I do, I just didn't know that you and all other dogs do too."

"*Well, we do, and so do other animals know. We're all parts of God just like people are.*"

"Yes! Yes you are! Summertime, do you ever see God when you go there?"

"*He's such a big bright light that you can't see anything else.*"

I was wondering if all species have a Big Someone to prepare them for Earth life, and as he often did,

Summertime responded to my thoughts. *"There's a teacher like Big Dog for every kind of animal. God picks the one that knows the most and can teach the rest."*

It was during one of our walks that I told him, "I know you like to go walking, Summertime."

"I LOVE to go walking! I love it next. First I love to eat."

"But you love Daddy and me, too."

"That's a different kind of love. That's the kind of love you FEEL. The other's the kind of love you DO."

Not all of our conversations were as serious as those. One day when I was bathing him in the shower with me—a frequent event that he wasn't fond of—I told him that as soon as we were finished, he would be beautiful. *"I don't see how. I'll just be wet."*

The psychic was right, Summertime never could be house-trained. The relentless trauma of his first home was hard-wired in his psyche where, unlike his emotions, it could not respond to love and caring attention. I told him that maybe he could stop messing in the house if he thought really hard about going outside at those times. *"I do think about it. I always try to remember, but every time I forget."* Often he said, *"I'm sorry I make extra work for you and I'm glad you know I can't help it."*

So I mopped the tile and vinyl floors daily and our carpet must have been the most frequently shampooed in the whole country. It was a small price to pay for having this dog who touched my very soul. In retrospect, I must have had that thought about Summertime or mentioned it to family and friends hundreds of times.

Summertime had become very frail, but since nothing was obvious—no vomiting or diarrhea or stiffness—I didn't know if he was hurting, so I asked him. *"Yes, I hurt."* "What hurts?" "*I hurt!*" X-rays showed nothing either, so continuing his diet and nutritional supplements was all we could do to keep him as healthy as possible while his body was simply wearing out.

When I was working at the computer, he spent most of his time sleeping near me, and now and then I would tell him in think-talk how much I love him—telepathy is a soul level connection and it registers during sleep the same way it does at a distance. Our attunement was so close that I took for granted our discussions that were so enlightening to me, but one time I was astounded.

As I glanced toward Summertime and told him silently "I love you," I saw a gold-colored cocker spaniel puppy rise from his body, linger a moment above him, then gradually fade. It had been two years since Summertime had been treated for that virulent infection that caused his deafness and the new vet on staff had said our dog would not live out the week. Except for the traumatic new affliction, he had rapidly rebounded, but now his health was clearly ebbing, and until I felt his slight breathing motion, I thought I had witnessed his transition from body into spirit.

He was still asleep when I left to start cooking dinner, still pondering that strange sight I had witnessed. A few minutes later he came into the kitchen and seemed unusually agitated. "Summertime, are you OK?"

"*No! I'm mad at you. You know about the puppy and it was supposed to be a surprise.*"

"What? Wasn't that a picture of you when you were a puppy?"

"*No! That's the puppy I'm going to send you someday, but now you know about it and you spoiled my surprise.*"

"But I don't know when you'll send the puppy, so it still

will be a surprise."

"Well, all right. I don't know when I can send it, and it won't be a tiny puppy, it will be a bigger dog that looks like me and needs a home here."

All of our dogs know that our home always is filled with spirits. To them, this is perfectly natural, and they know which spirits are human and which are dogs who used to live with us. So it was startling late one night soon after the "spoiled surprise" when Summertime, who had been sleeping in the bedroom when I left, was near hysteria when he ran into my office and cried, *"The spirits are trying to take me with them!"*

I got on the floor and held him close but his trembling didn't stop. I told him that he knows the spirits who come here are good and none would take him anywhere unless he wanted to go with them. *"This time there are too many and they came for me! Don't let them take me! I'm not ready to leave you!"* I turned off my computer and carried him to bed, where he slept in my arms all night.

A few nights later, August 9, 2004, I was rocking him, telling him over and over, it's time to go there and stay, you know I'll always love you. It was painful seeing him struggle so hard not to die, and after an hour, I put him in Bob's arms, where he peacefully breathed for a few seconds, then stopped. I had to leave Summertime so he could leave me.

During the night he wakened me to tell me, *"I LOVE it here!"* He said he can run around in his Summertime heavenly body or be within his Bigger Self, which is a big iridescent bubble of light that can go anywhere. The next morning when I told Bob what Summertime had said and how strongly I could feel him around me, my soul dog said, *"Well, I haven't left you!"*

Still, that afternoon the dogs, Bob and I were a sorrowful bunch walking along the roadside. Suddenly I had an unusual sensation, then saw an outline of blurred light the size of Summertime dashing up the hill past us. *"Yes, it's me. I want you to see me running like I used to. Now it's only love for us and no more cleaning for you."*

Two days later, as Bob and I were looking out our bedroom window, a young doe casually walked around the corner of the house, then stopped and looked in at us. Never before had a deer been within the fenced two acres— because of the trees and dense growth all along the outside of the seven-foot fence, there is no way they can leap over it. As Bob and I watched the beautiful doe calmly peering back at us from her spot only a few feet outside the window, Summertime told me that it was too soon for him to send us the puppy, so he sent a spirit deer. A minute or so later, the doe sauntered around the side of the house and out of sight.

Four dogs have found their way to us or vice versa since that day and none are cockers. In my occasional chats with Summertime, sometimes he tells me, without my asking, that it isn't yet the right time for the dog he wants to send us.

Osa

The first dog adoption day at our Humane Society shelter, early in 1994, already had started when the Animal Control Officer brought in a female right after picking her up, so she missed the thorough physical exam the other dogs had received. Although several families admired this friendly, self-assured, gleaming white-haired big girl of indeterminate age and heritage, all left without her and we brought her home to foster until the next monthly adoption event.

Her expressive brown eyes reflected her joy at riding with her head out the car window, and she eagerly trotted into the house and played her part in the usual canine greeting ceremony. Two hours later, she was sick. I called the emergency number for the weekend vet, who assured me it was only nervousness and she would get over it. She did not get better, and when the hospital opened Monday morning, I was there with a very sick dog. It took no more than a temperature reading for the diagnosis, parvo, and the prognosis: She's not going to make it through this.

She was put in isolation immediately and, like the hospital staff, I went through the sterilization procedures when I visited her twice daily during the ten days of her confinement. I called her Osa, Spanish for female bear—she looked like a young polar bear, one that was huddled and frightened. Each time I went to see her, I coaxed her to drink water, as the staff asked me to do, and later on I fed her

27

small bits of special food they gave me. I petted her while telling her I love her, please get well soon and come home with me.

The angel who kept her alive also protected our other dogs from that fiercely contagious and usually deadly disease. I brought this survivor home, a different dog from the proud one we first knew—Osa's self-confidence and zestful spirit were gone. Maybe that let us love her even more, and for the next eleven years she endeared her sweet self to family and friends and canine newcomers.

As she aged, her white hair turned tan and a large water sac developed behind each shoulder. Monica said they were not harmful, just unsightly, and neither she nor we wanted Osa to endure the discomfort of frequent draining procedures. She showed no signs of sickness when we left for a two-week trip to Italy, a combination of a speaking invitation for me and a family vacation.

All our dogs love their nanny JC, who lives in our home when we are away for more than a few hours and lets us leave with peace of mind, knowing that our fur family will have love and the best of care. The second week we were away, Osa started vomiting and JC took her to the hospital. The prescribed soft diet did not help, and there were four more trips for IVs to treat dehydration. Our wonderful nanny spent several hours during Osa's last night sitting beside her on the front deck, saying the same things Bob and I would have. When sleepiness overcame JC, she went to bed, and upon wakening a little later, she found Osa lying still on the foyer rug. That was the morning before we returned.

I looked at Osa's picture, an old one in the canine collage on my shelf, and silently told her I miss her and always will love her. Even though I knew think-talk during her last three years with us and she showed her pleasure when I talked with her that way, she never spoke to me. This time she did. *"I tried to wait for you, but I couldn't. I love you, Mommy,"* and she sent me her image—our beloved girl was once again fresh snowfall white and as sleek and poised as she had been the morning I met her.

Cloudy

The mostly-poodle we named Cloudy had an indomitable spirit like Summertime's and Osa's. His known history also started early in 1994, when the young woman who saw him limping along a California highway turned around to pick him up, not minding that he was soaked because of the downpour. He was weak from starvation— her veterinarian thought he was a malnourished whippet— and during his homelessness, his foreleg had been broken and healed crooked.

There is serendipity also about Cloudy joining our family. On Bob's return from a business trip, he ventured into the plane's kitchenette to request another cup of coffee and overheard a flight attendant telling her colleague about the dog she had found. She was trying to find him a home because he frightened her cat so much that she refused to come into the house. When Bob told her if that dog were 1000 miles north, he could live with us, Adriana said she would fly him up.

She called me to be sure I shared my husband's enthusiasm, and we made arrangements to meet three days later at the Portland, Oregon airport, the nearest to our home. Only after seeing our dogs, who did their usual sniffing jig around this stranger who looked like a huge pink spider, did Adriana tell us she had had second thoughts: Why would anyone be so eager to take in some dog sight unseen? Maybe we intended to sell it to a lab for medical experimentation, and that is why she asked her mother to accompany her. If they felt our motives were the least bit suspicious, there would be two of them to stand up to us and they would take the dog back to California. But as it turned out, all the dogs and dog lovers had a thoroughly delightful afternoon. Adriana visited us several times until her flight schedule changed a year later, and then we kept in touch by letters—mine included the most recent pictures of Cloudy and his buddies.

Cloudy was a misnomer until his fur grew enough to warrant the name. But even before he gained enough weight to look like a real dog, he was a digger without peer. No dirt within the fenced area was spared, and in time, his tight curls made snug containers for the little mud balls that covered him from head to tail. Dislodging those even with the shower going full blast was a Herculean chore—three baths in one day was the worst. This was several years pre-Sparkle, so I hadn't a clue what he was thinking during the first bath while I was muttering: I'm sick of bathing you every day, you've got to stop this asinine digging, I don't have time for this nonsense—mutter, mutter. Looking back, though, it is perfectly clear what he was thinking: *Where will I dig as soon as I get out of here?*

His penchant for digging didn't end with the leg operations, but his ability did. The first time he tore a meniscus, the surgeon said it would happen to the other one in six months, and almost to the day, it did. Cloudy never even winced during the two long uncomfortable recoveries. The same was true years later, when tumors were removed and his cheerful nature bounded back as soon as the anesthetic wore off.

The last seven of his fourteen years with us, when his fur was becoming mottled with tan on his face, back and legs, were post-Sparkle, and especially when Bob and I were taking our fur family for walks, Cloudy and I talked. Our neighborhood is the most ideal environment for dogs imaginable. The private hundred sixty-five acres and the surrounding hills are filled with tall evergreens and enough deciduous trees to make beautiful springs and autumns. With a meandering creek, beaver pond, and several areas where spring water flows, this is a haven for deer, rabbits, squirrels, moles and coyotes, all of whom leave the enticing smells that make walking along the curvy, little hill-and-dale road such a treat for dogs.

During our walks, Cloudy talked about his visits "there," where all animals are friendly, and when dogs visit, they play with the wild ones from the jungle too, because they aren't dangerous there. The children also play with all the animals and the big people know they are safe. Every place is beautiful and everyone is happy. People and animals who love each other never forget who they are; when they go there and stay, they can live together, but all the animals can go anywhere they want to because there aren't any fences.

All our fur family loved barking at Sierra and Rainy Day, llamas who live with Billy Goat on fenced acreage of flat land down the hill. Rainy Day was the only one who ever answered my Hello to each by name, and when he did, his response always was the same: *"Dogs are stupid. They are worthless. They only make noise. They need people to take care of them. We eat by ourselves."* No matter what I said—they are beautiful or our dogs were barking because they wanted to play or did they feel better since their winter coats had been clipped or did they like the apples we gave them—Rainy Day's comments didn't vary one whit. It is hard to imagine that Big Llama taught him to be so impudent, but who knows?

Like the other dogs, Cloudy didn't want to take his nose out of the wire fence and stop yelling at those three animals inside, but our walks' greatest attraction for him was Earth water. *"Earth water is much better because it has good things that pipe water doesn't have."* I already had heard a great deal about Big Dog, so it was no surprise that it was Big Dog who had told him this or that Cloudy added, *"All the water 'there' is Earth water."*

When I told Brillo, who joined our family about the same time as Cloudy, what his pal had said, his comment was: *"He always makes such a big deal about that. It's silly."* Nevertheless, he joined the others in drinking Earth water along the way. When we walked up the hill, they drank from the creek's little shallow pool at the bottom of a sloping bank, and when we went in the other direction, it was the spring water flowing along a slender grass-lined ditch.

One sunny afternoon when we took the route that includes the llamas and goat, Cloudy wasn't interested in stopping there and he didn't want to turn around at our regular place, before the hill that ends in a cul-de-sac at the top. *"I want to go all the way to the headwaters."*

"Cloudy, did you say *headwaters?*"

"Yes. That's where this water starts."

"That's far away from here, up in the mountains somewhere."

"I know *that's where the water starts. That's why I want to go there, so I can see it."*

Bob took the other dogs and started for home while

Cloudy and I continued walking almost to the top of the hill. When we turned around at the spot where the little ditch disappeared into the ground, he didn't say he was disappointed, but his body language did.

Even after he became too feeble to walk the full distance with the other dogs, he was determined to start out, and he did it with the same vigor as ever. He soon would slow to a moseying pace, then lie down and tell me when he couldn't go any farther. Bob or I would stay with him while one of us walked home with the other dogs and drove back to pick up Cloudy and whoever was with him. Only a few months later we had to do the same for Brillo, but his attitude was not nearly as appreciative as Cloudy's. Brillo said that since he is the boss of the dogs, it was only right that he should ride home.

Cloudy ate less and less of the food I prepared to tempt him and then stopped eating entirely. His last week was dreadful. Each morning my wakening thought was: Is Cloudy still alive? He had become so weak that he needed help to stand and teetered as he walked, but still he was adamant that he did not need his doctor's help to leave, he could do it himself. While I was caressing him on his last morning, July 1, 2008, he said, "*Sparkle and Big Dog told me it's not weak to have my doctor help me, so I'm ready to do that.*"

Always when both Bob and I are going out, I tell little Fruity—he had been in our family almost ten months—we are leaving so he won't be frightened when he barks and no one comes to see what he needs. This day I told him, "Daddy and I are taking Cloudy to his doctor and we'll be back soon." Fruity said, "*I know, and he's not coming back with you.*"

On these sad occasions when we take one of our fur kids to Monica's hospital for the last time, she sits on the floor with Bob and me and she pets and talks to whoever is with us. After hugging Cloudy and telling him what a good dog he is, she gave him the first of two shots. He lay peacefully with his head in my lap until he eased into his final sleep with the next injection. I was stroking him when I heard, *"I'm so happy, I'm so happy to be here!"* and he sent me an image of his young, robust body with its pristine white curls and he looked ever so proud of himself. Sparkle was standing beside him, and just as in the image she had sent me five months before, she was the slender, beautiful girl of her youth.

Brillo and Happy

Brillo was about two years old when he came to us and he stayed fourteen-and-a-half years, a few months longer than his mostly-poodle buddy.

Several days prior to our Humane Society chapter's second adoption day, Animal Control picked up this tall, long, lean stray. After the prerequisite medical exam that Osa missed, he joined the other homeless dogs who we hoped would be adopted by perfect families. But perhaps none of the people who were drawn to this quite striking dog were meant to have him, and I brought him home to foster until the next month's event.

He had a sprinkling of white around his nose and a dark reddish brown triangle above his black cheeks. The rest of his face was two-tone tan except the rings around his eyes, which matched the eyes' bittersweet chocolate color. His chest and belly were white and the rest of him was a dozen shades of auburn and brown. Regardless of its color, every single hair was bristly, like a really worn out scouring pad, so Brillo seemed an appropriate name for this fellow whose personality could be described as "Don't mess with me, I'm a Chicago street kid." No offense to Chicagoans—my husband lived there thirty-one years, and he's the one who came up with that idea. And when he was asked about Brillo's breed, Bob said he was a cross between a porcupine and a deer.

Yet there was a sophisticate beneath this dog-with-attitude. Brillo accepted handfed bites delicately and ate gracefully. He stood proudly, as if posing for a portrait, and he greeted visitors warmly, but not like the jumping jack he was well qualified to be. Those facets of his nature are why we took him to the crafts fair that advertised: Dogs on leashes welcome. As he walked among the people, many of whom stopped to pet him, with adults he was like a prince graciously acknowledging strangers' admiration, but when children came over, he was like a sweet little kid with them.

That outing was not long after the "fence incident" that cemented Brillo's place in our family. He had been our temporary lodger for only a few days when he was lying on the deck watching Bob build the sixty-foot long, nearly five-foot high cedar fence across the part of our property that can be seen from the road. After Bob finished, he said, "Well, Brillo, what do think of it?" Our foster fellow bounded across the yard and gracefully leaped over the fence with more than a foot of air between him and the top. The three-foot addition, which made "the fence that Brillo built" surely the oddest one anywhere, kept him from jumping. However, adding the same extra height to the wire fence already erected around the rest of the two enclosed acres didn't deter him one bit—he simply dug his way out.

According to our shelter's policies, a family can adopt a dog only if they can assure its safety. How many folks have a seven-foot fence mired in concrete? Probably because I was one of the founding members of our little chapter, there was no opposition to our adopting Brillo. Not only had he found a firm place in our hearts, but from the minute he walked through our door, he acted as if he had no doubt in the world that he was home. Furthermore, he acted as if he

37

was the Alpha Dog and none of our other fur kids objected.

Many years later, after I could think-talk, it was no surprise that he was the most outspoken of our family. It was about the time when Bob and I ordinarily would be getting out the leashes, but we were behind in preparing for dinner guests. The dogs started circling around and I told them we were too busy to go for a walk. In a disgusted tone, Brillo said, *"That's not fair!"* "Oh, come on, Brillo—you have all that space out there to run around and play." *"This place is a prison with that fence!"*

He had told me often enough that Cloudy's yapping annoyed him, but one day his objection came in the form of a thunderclap. When I told him to stop, he was just making Cloudy bark louder, he said, *"Well, he pisses me off."* "Brillo! I can't believe you said that!" *"You and Daddy say it all the time."*

It was later, though, when he told me that it is from people's conversations and thoughts that he learns words and when to use them. He said Big Dog teaches dogs to listen carefully when people talk and to pay attention to what they think because they don't always say what they really mean. Another of Big Dog's instructions to him was not to start a fight, but if another animal did, he had to fight bravely. Brillo said he takes his boss dog job seriously, but he doesn't have to be mean to do it because all the dogs mind him.

Now that I knew about "fight bravely," I understood that when Happy had challenged him for that Alpha slot some years before, Brillo was well primed to be a warrior when he had to be.

*   *   *

Happy's coming into our family was still another bit of serendipity. As Dog Chairman, I was very active in our chapter's operations but rarely at the shelter because it was large enough only for cats—homeless dogs had to be fostered until they could be adopted. So it was four dogs' good fortune that I stopped by the shelter just as the Animal Control Officer, a soft-hearted young man, came in and said he hated having to take these dogs to the pound in Vancouver—it was full and all incoming animals would be euthanized. He felt especially bad about the little female whose fourteen years with a family came to an end because she didn't fit into their elegant new home. Could I possibly foster her and maybe the others too?

I brought her home along with two medium-sized dogs and an English mastiff-Saint Bernard youngster. I quickly found good homes for three of the dogs—that dear little old lady lived with our neighbors, who were attentive to all her needs until she died two years later—but from my recent trials finding the right family for a Great Dane we had fostered, I knew that few families could manage a 70-pounder who wasn't even half grown.

Our dogs accepted this big auburn and white stranger with an oversized head and immense paws the way they did each newcomer—a lot of circling around, wagging tails and smelling rears, and then the tacit OK, you can stay. So we named him Happy, Bob doubled the size of the doggie door, and he and our newest adoptee adored each other from the get-go. Thankfully, Happy quickly learned that his bathroom was not in the house or on the deck, because by the day the rest of this big lovable boy grew to catch up with his head and paws. A year or so after he joined our family, he easily got the blue ribbon for largest dog in the show—he was triple the size of the red ribbon winner.

It wasn't until Happy weighed 220 pounds and looked like a lion walking through the house that he must have decided his size entitled him to rule the clan. Whatever his reasoning was—it was before I knew mind-talk and during one of Bob's two-week business trips—one day, without any warning, he lit into 65-pound Brillo. Apparently the outcome changed nothing, because two days later he did it again. Those fights were in the kitchen, several minutes of wild gyrations with snarling and biting that ended as suddenly as they started, then both dogs warily eyed each other as they walked in separate directions.

The third time Happy struck, the battle was ferocious. They chased throughout the house, tossing saliva and dripping blood in every room. My pouring a bucket of water over them didn't faze either dog, it just made a bigger mess for me to clean later. They continued battling for what seemed to me like a lifetime and stopped only when both dropped from exhaustion near the chair where I had sat down, feeling helpless to do anything except pray. They needed antibiotics and lots of stitches, and maybe because Happy's wounds were worse, that ended the issue of who was boss. Although they never became bosom buddies, they buried the hatchet.

Other than those instances, Happy was sweet, affectionate, playful and a show-stopper at the hospital when we took him for check-ups. Monica had seen his early symptoms of both afflictions that affect dogs his size. Their weight is too much for their hearts and bones to handle— they die of heart failure or bone cancer and their usual life span is six or seven years. Happy seemed healthy and vibrant, and medication was relieving his stiffness, but he left us when he was not yet five.

At that time Bob often traveled and he enjoyed feeding the dogs when he was home. They all would follow him to the kitchen and lie near their elevated dinner racks, giving the daddy of the house their full attention and probably crediting him with Best Quality Time. When he called out "Dinnertime," Happy always came to look for me, then we would walk together back to the kitchen with my arm around his neck. That's where we were going when he collapsed, whimpered once, and was still. We scattered his ashes, like those of the dogs who had passed on before him, over the land all of them had happily roamed.

Happy was a joyous part of our life for over four years, and his place in our hearts isn't diminished an iota by including him in Brillo's story as the lone challenger for Alpha Dog status.

*   *   *

From Brillo's first days with us—and a big clue that he had come to stay—he slept on Bob's and my bed. More than a decade later, when his joints were becoming stiff, he started spending most of the day there, too, usually lying on my pillow, as if it were his throne. One afternoon when I walked into the bedroom and greeted him, I was wondering if the other dogs still regarded him as their boss. He said, *"They know I'm the boss wherever I am."*

As macho as he was, or maybe pretended to be, he was sensitive to the plight of Fruity, the dear old black and white Lhasa apso who was part of our family during Brillo's last year. Fruity couldn't hear anything except shrill barks or gunshots on TV and his vision was limited to seeing large forms silhouetted against strong light. Observing the little guy walking straight into our 60- to 90-pounders, Brillo told me, *"He can't see anything. I have to protect him so they won't tramp on him."* Well, I never saw him running interference, so maybe he told the big dogs never to growl when Fruity bumped into them.

We often had spoken about the spirits in the house, and it finally occurred to me to ask Brillo what they look like. *"They're balls of light and some are bigger or brighter than others. Sometimes they move around, but they don't make any noise."* One night he told me there was a huge golden light ball and many small ones, some of which flickered. He was surprised that I have never seen them, and I didn't think to ask why Big Dog doesn't tell the puppy souls that most people can't see spirits.

The two cockapoos who live up the hill irritated Brillo no end. They often ran down their long driveway when we walked by and signaled their proprietary rights by making a yappy little ruckus. Every time we encountered them, Brillo and I had the same conversation: He said those dogs are ridiculous. I said they're protecting their property. He said they don't know how. One afternoon after we passed that driveway and its noisy little guardians, he made a quick U-turn and started back. "Brillo, what are you doing?" *"I told you they don't know how to protect their property. They need to do it right and I'm going back there to train them."* He still had attitude, but he had become more thoughtful, and it seemed to me, introspective.

His face and legs had turned white, his arthritic ankles had become wildly pigeon-toed, and his hindquarters were painfully stiff, so it was a struggle for him to get up on the bed. Since that was where he spent most of his time, it was where our serious conversations took place, often after everyone else was sleeping. When I lightly rubbed his swollen joints, he told me they hurt. Yes, he knew we were giving him medicine, but still his legs and backside hurt a lot. He said he couldn't remember much of his life before coming to us—or maybe he didn't want to talk about it. He summed it up: *"I got along OK. It's much better here."*

During his life with us, he had bid farewell to seven of our dear dogs who "had gone there to stay," but it was only after Cloudy died that he started to talk about his leaving someday too. *"Will you miss me?"* "Oh, Brillo, you *know* we will!" *"It's better living there because nobody is sick or fights. But I'm still having a good time here and I'm not ready to leave."* He didn't want to miss out on walks, starting with the group and riding back home; he ate with gusto; and occasionally grumped enough to let the others know he still was head of the fur family. So never mind that probably he had passed his seventeenth birthday, I thought of him as indestructible, like his spirit always had been.

I think Cloudy's leaving is what broke Brillo's spirit. I was lying beside him, telling him for the thousandth time that he is the best boss dog ever and I love him, and he said, *"I miss Cloudy. He was my best friend."* I told him that Cloudy visits him here and when he visits there, he can see Cloudy. *"It's not the same as having him here all the time."* When I reminded him that he used to be annoyed by Cloudy's barking, he said, *"That's just the kind of dog he is and I got over that a long time ago."*

One night I asked, "Do you see Summertime when you're visiting there?"

"*Sometimes I talk to him, but usually he's too busy to play because he's one of Big Dog's assistants.*"

We talked a bit about what an important job that is, and then I asked, "Brillo, do you ever see Katy?"

*   *   *

For about eighteen months Katy, the golden cocker spaniel our friends rescued when she was middle-aged, lived with us during their frequent travels. She had stopped eating when her companion Bobby, a wonderful chocolate Lab, died, and when I heard that her family soon would leave for a three-week trip, I asked them to let her stay with us rather than in a boarding kennel. I would have done that even if Katy hadn't reminded me so much of Summertime. The big difference was that she did not like to be petted and he had mellowed into a lap dog and profuse kisser.

But beneath Katy's aloofness there was a romantic element, and right off the bat she developed a crush on Brillo. He wasn't flattered by her mild attentions. "*Why is she here? She's just a nuisance.*" When she was with us, so were her two beds, one in our bedroom and the other in the foyer, and when Bob and I were in our room, like all the other dogs, Katy was too. That's where she was when I went to the kitchen, and when I came out a few minutes later, she was lying in her foyer bed.

"Katy, let's go back to the bedroom now."

"*I can't.*"

"Why not?"

"*Brillo said he doesn't want me there.*"

But by the end of that visit, it was plain that he had warmed to our visitor. When I told her, "Katy, Brillo is being nicer to you, isn't he?" she answered, *"He doesn't talk to me very much, but what he says is nice."*

One morning her real mommy called and asked us to bring Brillo when we went to their home for dinner that evening—she wanted to see him and Katy together. I told Brillo he must not tell our other dogs where we were going because it would hurt their feelings that they couldn't go. When Lone Invitee, Bob and I went to the door, it was natural that the rest of the dogs clustered there too. But they were accustomed to only one or two of them going with us in the car, and since that usually was to their hospital, it was more like "Goodbye, poor you," and the others don't try to rush out the door. This time they all did. When we got them back in the house, Cloudy was their spokesdog: *"Brillo told us he's going to Katy's party. It's not fair that she invited only him. We want to go too."*

It was bad enough that he snitched, it was worse that once at "Katy's party," he ignored her. I know only what dogs tell me, never what they say to each other, so I had to ask, "Katy, is Brillo saying nice things to you tonight?" *"He's not talking to me at all."* When I told him he was being rude and mean, he said, *"This is her house and she should be treating me special."*

However, before that evening's cavalier behavior, he had let her wiggle into his affections. One night during her first visit, when the whole gang had gathered around at bedtime, he told me she could sleep on the bed with him and Cloudy so she wouldn't be scared. So Katy's romance may have been lopsided, but it wasn't totally unrequited, and it continued until she died peacefully in her own home two years ago.

*　　*　　*

Brillo hadn't answered my question, so I asked again, "When you visit there, do you ever see Katy?"

"*Sometimes. She's different.*"

"What do you mean, different? Doesn't she remember you?"

"*Yeh, she knows me.*"

"Then what's different?"

There was a pause before he told me, "*She sort of grew up.*" I didn't press him further. I simply assumed that she had met a handsome hairy gentleman who always treated her respectfully.

More than a few times during our bedtime talks, Brillo said, "*I'm getting old. I can't do what I used to.*" Maybe he was thinking that he no longer could dig out under the wire fence and run across the road to see his best friend and bring him back home. Duke was a splendid border collie, an "only child," and he enjoyed playing with our crowd. But after his daddy's diligent don't-chase-cars training was undone time and again by Brillo, a master chaser, Duke's safety was assured by one of those collars that gives mild shocks when the dog goes beyond the invisible fence. From then on until dear Duke's lifetime ended, our wanderer went to visit his buddy, and afterwards he went exploring lord only knows where until he was ready to sit silently on the terrace outside the kitchen window until Bob or I noticed him and opened the door so he could come in.

Whatever he did on the outside, *getting there* was the game. His record was three times in one day, with Bob or me searching for the newest hole and blocking it after each escapade. After Duke died, Cloudy became Brillo's best friend. I'll bet they collaborated on creating the escape routes because frequently both of them got out and went touring, and occasionally Alpha Dog even persuaded all of his siblings to follow him. Rounding up the group was a chore I was glad to call history when Brillo's arthritic joints halted his adventures, long after Cloudy's leg operations ended any digging partnership they may have had.

Now, not only was Brillo admitting to aging, but he no longer howled when Bob and I left together. It was soon after he came into our family that the neighbor with an "ornery cuss" reputation stopped by to complain that Brillo chased his motorcycle, and if we didn't keep him inside the fence, he would report us. After I explained our dilemma about our dog's escape routes, the man said he also sounded like a coyote baying at the moon and it was annoying. That was the first we knew that our new fellow made any sound at all when we were out, but hundreds of times since then, I have gotten out of the car and gone back into the house to tell him, "Brillo! Pul-ease! I asked you not to yell!"

Maybe by *"I can't do what I used to,"* he meant he no longer could run like a gazelle with my daughter Betsy. Her home was in Panama, and when she brought her four children during school vacations or holidays, she took him running with her early in the morning while everyone else was still asleep. As Brillo aged, their outings became jogging, then walking fast a short distance, then sauntering an even shorter distance. But it was as Brillo said, *"It's still exclusively me she takes with her."*

He knew Betsy was coming soon. *"Tell her I'm old now and can't walk very well."* I told him she couldn't either because of a knee injury and they were a good pair. She was here for his last three days, but instead of their last walk, it was their final goodbye. I think Brillo waited for her before telling me, "*I can't stay here any longer. I need my doctor to help me go.*"

The same animal hospital, the same sad routine. But afterwards, what an exhilarated Brillo greeted me! "*They knew I was coming and had a party ready with balloons and food and everything! All my friends are here and other animals I don't know, and lots of children. Now watch me run!*" He left the crowd I saw in the image he was sending— Cloudy, Sparkle, Summertime, Osa and many other dogs, a lot of little children, a few adults and some large animals, and yes, a sea of balloons—and his strong, youthful body leaped in the air, then ran out of sight.

I don't think anyone who met Brillo ever forgot him. He was special to all our family, friends who visited have asked about him throughout the years, and neighbors expressed sympathy for our loss. He left a void in our home that never can be filled when he died November 3, four months after his special pal Cloudy and nine months after Sparkle. Knowing how happy and active they are in their fabulous world eases the sorrow and our missing them. And our other dogs, who had been emotionally affected by the dying energy, then the absence of their companions, needed uplifted spirits from Bob and me so they could feel secure.

Jessie

Jessie was six-and-a-half years old the summer of 2006 when an acquaintance told me about overhearing the man tell the receptionist at the Humane Society in Vancouver why he had brought his dog. She had been with him since she was two months old and he didn't want to give her up, but his new job meant a great deal of traveling and there was no one to care for her. My acquaintance, an animal lover who lived in a rental house and could have only cats, had seen Jessie looking bewildered as she was led away from her man who was in tears. Could I please help Jessie somehow?

The woman at the Humane Society said I could spend time with the dog in the outdoor fenced enclosure, but she couldn't be adopted until she "was socialized." We found the cage with JESSIE printed on a small card attached to the door and a sad-looking golden Labrador lady lying against the far wall. She slowly stood up to be leashed, then reluctantly followed the volunteer, who said I could see for myself why this dog needed a great deal of socialization before she could be adopted.

How could these people not understand that Jessie was dealing with confusion about why her man was crying when he left her in this strange place where all the other dogs were frightened just like she was? I wanted to take every one of them home with me, and Jessie did come. Apparently a few minutes with me was enough to socialize her. I filled out pages of papers, paid $150—that included the cost of still another collar and leash, but it is for a good cause—and Jessie and I walked out into the sunshine.

When we reached home, it took maybe two minutes for that so recently desolate dog to morph into a whirlwind. She dashed around the house; darted in and out of the doggie door; ran through the brush, trees and boulders on the front slope, then up the hill to the denser growth at the back. It isn't that the other dogs didn't accept her, it's that she is the quintessential puppy in a 90-pound body and there was no way they could keep up with her. Bob and I had the same thought: Jessie needs a little boy or a young dog with the same vitality. A child was out of the question and we had our hands full with four old dogs who needed a great deal of attention and now this livewire—Jessie would have to make do without a playmate as zany and active as she.

A few days after she came, I wrote a long letter to her former daddy—the woman who handled the adoption was pleased that I wanted to do that and said she would personally see that it reached him. I fudged when I wrote that Jessie fit perfectly into our fur family, but the rest of my letter was true: The wonderful doctor our dogs had; the raw food diet they thrived on, plus special treats; the little private road where we take them walking; the fenced land for their safety; and that Jessie would be loved and cared for all her life.

Good Will is a wonderful source of small lightweight blankets, and I found a vividly multicolored one for Jessie. She interpreted "This is your blanket, Jess" to mean whatever she wanted to do with it, and she ripped it apart to make a bunch of pull toys that she brought to Bob or me. When all of those were destroyed, she made more from her second blanket, and the sturdy octopus toy that Betsy bought for her met the same fate.

Jessie is even more of a menace with paper. Our waste baskets—quite charming unique styles—stand empty, useless except for the two that are hiding lamp cords. She has chewed up letters, bank statements, book and magazine covers, napkins, Kleenex, toilet paper, my Do NOW lists, greeting cards, bills, checks, cereal boxes—anything that got its start when a tree was cut down.

The list of destruction includes my printout of the introduction and topics to discuss with the guest on my radio show—I discovered it in scraps on the floor two minutes before airtime. Since then I try to remember to close my office door each time I leave the room. Blocking Jessie's path to my stacks of paper motivated her to go upstairs to Bob's loft office, where she found a satisfying new pastime. She crawled under the desk, pulled out the paper shredder and knocked off its top—whatever bits she didn't eat on the spot or strew all over the carpet, she brought downstairs for later noshing. Now there is an expandable gate across the top of the steps.

We have to ask, what is missing from her diet that she's supplementing by eating every paper she can get in her mouth? Maybe nothing, because she also gnaws on pens, blocks of wood, contents of ashtrays, indoor plants and plastic food containers. She killed the reading glasses that were on my bedside table and wounded my crossword calculator. Not long ago, Bob put a full mug of eggnog on the table between our bedroom easy chairs—Jessie was there in a flash. She slurped most of it and splashed the rest on the TV remote, fortunately not enough to drown it.

As I am writing, she is by my side tearing into chunks an old beach towel. We haven't been back to Good Will to get a third blanket and that towel was her nighttime cover. These kids don't really need a cover—they just go along with what *I* need, that extra little flourish of tucking them in while telling them I love them and now it's bedtime.

I would love to know what churns in the mind of our perpetual puppy, who welcomes each morning as if she had drunk six cups of coffee, but Jessie is as uncommunicative as she is demonstrative. I'm glad we followed Betsy's recent recommendation to get *Marley and Me*. We just finished reading this wonderful book and now we're grateful for what Jessie doesn't do. We also are thankful that she enlivens our home and keeps us smiling even without ever saying a word to me about anything.

Apple

Exactly a year after Jessie came, we made a 550-mile round trip to pick up Apple. Her mother sent me an email about lodging for the three-day conference where I would be speaking, and after she read *Matthew, Tell Me about Heaven*, she wrote often, asking questions about the sick mother she knew who was concerned about her little boy in custody of his father, an evil man who had the money and power to never again let her see their son. Juliette wanted to know, if that mother dies, can her love reach the boy from Heaven and keep him safe from his father's dark influence? When she asked if she could pay us to keep Apple, her affectionate, vivacious, well-mannered, stocky, ten-year-old Rottweiler, for two weeks while she went on vacation, I wrote back that we would love to do that for no charge at all. She didn't reply.

When Bob and I arrived at the conference, we learned from the leader that Juliette had gone to the Oregon coast, where she ended her life, and Apple was with a woman in northern California. We discovered that all of us had a piece of the puzzle, but we didn't know each other so we couldn't put the pieces together. I knew Juliette's concerns about her sick friend's little boy if that friend died. The conference leader knew Juliette's ex-husband had custody of their young son and she didn't have even visiting rights, and she despaired about being separated from the boy. The woman with whom she left Apple felt something was amiss when she brought the dog's two beds, ear medication, shampoo, brushes and combs, leashes, towels, sheets and nail clippers for only a two-week stay.

We arranged to meet the temporary caretaker in a quiet park by a river near the Oregon-California border and we took Jessie, hoping the two dogs would play and Apple would feel comfortable about coming home with us. Apple didn't play. She showed no interest at all in Jessie, who was romping around, or in Bob or me during the hour we sat with the woman who took her there. But when we stood up to leave, Apple walked to our car instead of to the small truck in which she had been riding the previous month.

Maybe because our dogs are accustomed to others visiting and sometimes staying, or more likely because they were too sleepy when we got home in the wee hours of the morning, there was no fanfare when Apple walked in with us. She looked around, got a drink, and settled in as a somber loner. She and Brillo weren't fond of each other—maybe she signaled that she was used to being an only dog and submissive to none—but except for the occasional growl, their tepid relationship didn't bother the other dogs.

Apple did not like to be hugged, and despite my telling her often each day that she's my Apple angel, I am so happy she's with us and I want her to be happy here, she waited a full year before saying a word. One night when I was putting her blanket over her, I told her, "Apple baby, please, please be happy." She said, *"I'm as happy as I can be. I know what happened to my mother."* She didn't talk again for several months, but during the bedtime ritual, she started putting her nose in my hand or rolling over so I could rub her belly.

It was soon after Brillo left that she spoke the second

time. Occasionally when I finished working late at night, I would find her sleeping behind my chair, but this night when she came in she brushed against my arm to let me know she was here. "Hello, my Apple Angel."

"I like it when you call me that. I know what angels are."

"Oh, Apple, I'm SO glad you're talking to me! I want you to be happy."

"I know you do. Sometimes I am."

"Do you see your other mommy when you visit there?"

"Yes. Sometimes she's happy and sometimes she's sad."

"Is that why sometimes you are sad?"

"Yes."

Slowly the wall Apple built around her heart is coming down. Perhaps she never again will be the vivacious dog she was with Juliette, who may always be her only real mother, but she is becoming the affectionate lady that her mother knew.

Babe

It was nearly midnight and we were almost home after attending an Oregon Symphony concert, the last of their 2008 season. About a mile down the little road that dead ends in our neighborhood, we saw a big dog walking slowly in the direction we were headed. Bob stopped and I got out, calling "Come, baby." The dog walked to our car and jumped into the back seat as quickly as if he had done it all his life.

He had no collar, so all we knew was what we could see: an overweight, dingy gray and black male with sad brown eyes. It was too late to introduce him to our dogs, so I made a bed for him in the garage and left the door open enough so he could get out. After drinking a bowl of water and eating two cans of food and an assortment of biscuits—that's when I discovered that his upper and lower front teeth were missing—he lay down on the blankets and closed his eyes.

When I opened the kitchen door in the morning, he was sitting so close that our dogs had to walk around him as they went out en masse to check out this newest stranger. He must have passed their critique because they all came in and ate biscuit and meat breakfast together. Afterwards, when I told this big fellow I was going to try to find his family, he said, "*Please let me stay here.*" My heart sank. It was not a good time to add any more dynamics to the fur family. They already were nervous because they knew Cloudy was dying, and I wanted to spend extra time with him, not less because a stray dog also needed attention.

I named him Babe because he had responded immediately to "Come, baby"—I figured he deserved that little bit of continuity in his life. The first vacancy at the hospital was the next day, but the groomer could squeeze him into her schedule if I took him right away. And what a transformation I picked up a few hours later—he was sturdy, not fat, and his black and white hair glistened—so it was a handsome Babe that Bob took to be examined. The vet said he was a healthy seven- or eight-year-old border collie mix, and his teeth weren't missing; they had been ground down to nubs probably from a long time of chewing on a heavy chain.

Babe is the epitome of canine gentlemanliness. His first morning in our family he followed the others out the doggie door, gingerly took food from my hand, chose two living room chairs as his napping spots, and was abundantly affectionate. It was hard to reconcile all that with the ground-down teeth, but I had no time to talk with him until after Cloudy left us, a week later.

Our first conversation came soon afterwards, when I asked Babe if he lived nearby. *"I don't think so. I walked a long, long time and was so tired that I wanted to stop, but Big Dog told me to keep on walking and I would find the right home."* Maybe Big Dog knows us. Anyway, from everything I have heard about him, dogs pay attention to what he tells them.

It was perhaps a week later when Babe told me more about himself. His first family loved him and took him for long rides in the country. One time when they stopped and he finished exploring, he ran and ran looking for them but couldn't find them. He was too tired to keep on looking and it was dark so he stopped at a house where the people fed him and let him stay. I asked if he got lost again, like he did with his first family. "*No, I finally got away. They didn't hurt me, but they didn't care anything about me.*" Other than that tale of his life before Big Dog directed him our way, Babe has said very little—he seems completely happy with frequent hugs and love rubs and romping with Jessie.

After more than two years living with dogs who had no interest at all in participating in her hyperactivity, Jessie finally had a playmate. Right off, Babe reacted to her swinging the thick knotted rope dangling from her jaws by grabbing the other end and the tug-of-war was on. After the rope was in fragments, Jessie's beach towel cover served the same purpose, and sometimes they just dash around the house, their tails wagging like missiles.

Babe is the only male in our Big Three, but he is far too mild-natured to be Alpha Dog, whereas Apple's disposition is perfectly suited, and after Brillo left, she slid naturally into that role. Probably Jessie, in her eternal puppyhood, doesn't even know what an Alpha Dog is, and Fruity has been in his own little world ever since he came into our family.

Fruity

Long after other responsibilities had limited my involvement with our local shelter to only fund-raising activities, it had expanded to accommodate a few dogs. Early in September 2007, one of the volunteer veterinarians told me about the black and white Lhasa apso, the worst case of neglect the staff had ever seen, whom they called Marty and estimated to be about thirteen. He had been receiving medical care ever since he had been found wandering around in the street two months before, and he needed still more minor surgeries. However, nothing could restore his vision or hearing, and those handicaps plus his chronic skin condition and the expensive eye drops he needed twice daily for the rest of his life made him the worst possible candidate for adoption they could imagine.

Nine days later Marty was well enough for me to bring him and his eight medications home. I am not waving some do-gooder banner here—I was unabashedly self-serving. Having Marty to take care of was like more time with Lucky, the tiny black and white fellow who walked into my life September 11, 1998, the day that would have been my son Matthew's thirty-sixth birthday. I was driving along a stretch of nearly deserted pasture land, taking two of our dogs for dental appointments, and suddenly a little fur ball walked into the middle of the road. I braked, jumped out, scooped him up and waved a thank-you to the approaching driver who had screeched to a halt.

I left my new passenger and his unholy odor at the hospital to be examined and bathed. When I returned, I learned that he had been matted to the skin, where a colony of fleas were thriving; he was probably ten to twelve years old; was blind in one eye and had severely distorted vision in his deformed eye; and his ears were infected. As I paid the unexpectedly high bill, the office manager said, "He's sure one lucky dog that you found him," and I came home with two dogs whose teeth were sparkly and a little guy whose hair was gone but so were the fleas, and several bottles of meds for him.

Our six dogs kept us very busy, and I had given Bob my word that I would not add to our family. So when I walked in cradling that squirming little body, who could blame my husband for saying this isn't fair, I had promised him I never would do this again. This is different, I told him—this is Lucky, Matthew's birthday gift to me for being his mother. It took Bob perhaps as long as half an hour to feel as grateful as I that this dear little dog had come into our lives.

Lucky was shy and sweet, the quietest dog imaginable, and totally content to lie in a lap or find his own spot, and we adored him for the two-and-a-half years left of his life. He was by far the smallest dog I had ever had, and I thought of him as a baby who needed a mother's care. He never was sick, so it was a shock when he died an hour after Bob and I returned from an evening class. I wasn't ready for Lucky to leave, and when I met Marty nine years after that morning when a miniature version of himself walked into the road in front of my car, I felt thankful for more time with dear little soul Lucky.

That really warped thinking blew right out of my head

about a nanosecond after Marty came home with me. Our fur family seemed puzzled when I put him on the floor, as if he were some alien life form whose little black and white rear didn't merit the usual check-me-out routine. They just stood there, towering over him, as Marty confidently walked under Brillo and kept on going. I steered him into the guestroom, hugged him and told him to stay there, I would be right back. I spoke aloud to the other dogs, but it seemed more natural to think-talk with a nearly deaf little fellow and usually that's what I did.

I took him his quota of pills for that time of day, each disguised in a little bite of his special canned food, and put the dish right under his nose. "Marty, here are some special treats for you." "*Where?*" He couldn't smell either. After he ate, he said, "*Marty isn't my real name and I don't like it.*"

"Oh, OK. What is your real name?"

"*Billy. I don't like it either.*"

"What name would you like?"

"*Fruity. I like the ooooo sound in my head.*"

His chronic skin condition required a bath with medicated soap twice a week. Our oversized kitchen sink and flexible spray faucet would be ideal, and after collecting a wash cloth, towels and his shampoo, I gathered up Fruity and told him what was in store for him. "*Am I stinky? I don't like to be stinky,*" and while I was bathing him: "*I love this. I love my bath. I love warm water.*"

I wrapped him in towels, carried him to our bathroom and turned on the hair dryer. "*I love the whizzer best of all.*" I put him down and steered him out of the bathroom into our room, then turned him toward the hallway. "*Am I going back to my room now?*" His room? Well, now it seemed practical to feed him there. "*I love my dinner. It's delicious.*"

Afterwards he sat perfectly still while I put drops in his eyes, and he said "*Thank you*" when I gave him a little biscuit for dessert.

I had been holding up my end of our brief conversations and my words hadn't posed any problem. "Fruity, do you have to go outside now?"

"*Why?*"

"Do you need to go out to … um … do your business, go to the toilet?"

"*What?*"

"Um … oh, do you have to do potty?"

"*Oh. You mean one poo and two poo.*"

That taken care of, I got the big lightweight neon orange blanket I had bought for him and folded it until it became a mattress for the large soft baby basket I felt so fortunate to find on sale at an antique shop. I put Fruity on top and told him this was the bed especially for him. He turned around a few times, then jumped out. After the third time, I doubled the blanket, spread it on the carpet at the foot of the bed and put him on it. He saw me as a big blob, but somehow he could detect what was beneath him: "*Thank you for my beautiful blanket.*" He curled up and went to sleep.

An hour later when I passed the guestroom, he was sitting up and looking out into the hall. I didn't want him to feel abandoned, so I steered him out of his room, around the corner and down the hallway into the master bedroom, which is large enough for a leisure area with a bookshelf, two comfortable chairs, small tables and a large old wooden chest that holds our television. I placed Fruity in Bob's lap, where he stayed for the rest of the evening and watched the TV screen change from light to dark. When he fell asleep, I took him back to his room, and he spent his first night there on his beautiful blanket. At 7:30 a.m., he barked for the first time. If his body were commensurate with his vocal volume, he could be an elephant.

Fruity learned amazingly quickly how to navigate his way throughout the house, and after only a couple of lessons, he mastered the doggie door between the kitchen and the front deck and the two steps from the deck to the yard. After that, whenever nature called, he could make those trips himself and always upon returning went straight to the water dish to reload.

His chronic skin condition requires keeping his hair short, so there are fairly frequent trips to the groomer and in between, a lot of home baths. The first deluded me into thinking they always would be gleeful times. However, a professional grooming came soon after that, and his second bath at home was a litany of complaints: The water's too warm, now it's too cold, I got his face wet, the water's too high, I'm taking too long, when will I finish, I got his face wet again, that's enough! The whizzer he loves best didn't fare any better—it touched him, he's tired of standing still, when will this stop, it touched him again, he's dry enough, and he wants all his baths at the other place. Well, if I can't take him there every time, I need to get a big box that has a whizzer outside so he can move around or sleep while he gets dry.

One day he didn't stop at griping. He kept turning around in the sink, climbed up on the counter, soaking the towel there, and shook like a dervish before I could get my hands on the second towel. When I was blow-drying him in the bathroom, he thrashed around until he squirmed out of my hands and knocked both porcelain soap dishes—safely out of his normal reach—and an electric toothbrush on the floor. The toothbrush survived and I caught the thrasher just before he landed. "Fruity, why have you been so awful today?" *"It comes naturally."*

I figured out that keeping a conversation going throughout bath time reduced his complaints and scrambling around. One day I told him having a bath was like being in a little swimming pool. *"What is that?"* I told him a pool has lots of water, like a pond, but not as much water as a river or a lake, and I asked if he knows what those are. *"No, I don't get involved in those."* "Oh, OK." *"What is swimming?"* "It's playing in a lot of water and lots of dogs like to do it." *"I'm not one of them."*

It was a gloomy all-day drizzle, and when Fruity came inside after strolling around on the deck—his rainy day bathroom—and taking his time to do both poos, I plunked him in a sinkful of warm water. After talking about the weather, I asked if he had gotten very wet while he was outside. *"No, I am wet because you are washing me."*

However, one of the days when his skin problem had flared up and daily baths were necessary, I had a dreadful headache and didn't talk to him at all. But he was so still throughout the double wash and rinse cycle that it seemed as if I'd been bathing a stuffed animal. I told him how good he had been and thanked him.

"I was good because I know you hurt."

"How do you know that?"

"I feel it."

"You can feel my head hurting?"

"I feel YOU. Dogs know when people hurt."

"Does Big Dog teach you that?"

"No, we feel it naturally. Big Dog teaches us to be thoughtful and kind when people hurt."

When I was drying him after his first bath following a grooming session, I told him, "The whizzer works better since you had your hair cut." *"The whizzer works the same. My haircut is what is better."*

He had emptied his bladder and bowels before we started off to the groomer's one sunny afternoon, but a few minutes into the drive, the car suddenly smelled like a baby's freshly filled diaper. "Fruity, do you have to do more two poo?" *"Yes! Can't you smell that big gaslet?"*

After Bob and I took the big dogs for their walk, one of us would take Fruity out on his little bright blue leash. His first stop was the car tire, where he did one poo, then over to the grass for two poo, and after each act, he announced what he had just done. When he was through milling around on the grass, he'd head down the driveway into the road, crossing back and forth until Bob's or my patience gave out.

One day when I started to put on his leash, Fruity rebelled. *"I don't want the rope. I don't like it when you pull me."* I explained again that it's to protect him from cars so he won't get hurt. *"I don't care. I don't want the rope."* So I carried him to the front yard, which until then had been only for supervised toilet time. Had he been allowed to meander without any watchful eye, he could wander for hours through the dense brush down the front slope or up the back hillside before we could find him.

This day I watched him travel around in the patch of grass between the bark-covered area in front of the deck and the path along the bushes that the big dogs had made. After about ten minutes or more exploring in a big circle, he made his way back toward the steps, jumped up on the deck, said, *"That was a good roam,"* and went inside through the doggie door. After a few more days of seeing him circulate within the same perimeters and confidently return, I felt that he was safe out there on his own. I stopped watching him and Bob started calling him The Little King.

Several mornings after the "good roam," I walked with Fruity into his room after his outing because I wanted to see his reaction when he noticed that his blanket and the flocoti rug that were there when he left no longer were. *"Where is my beautiful blanket? Where is my beautiful rug?"* weren't casual questions—he sounded frantic. I told him I was washing them and all the other dogs' blankets too. He sounded so relieved when he said, *"That's good. Nothing in this house should be stinky."*

Especially not with visitors coming for the weekend. I told our little fellow that two very nice people were going to sleep with him in his room that night. *"Oh, no! Oh, no!"* So he slept with Brillo, Cloudy, Bob and me, and ever since then, this has been Fruity's nighttime place.

A couple of days later I got him a small bright aqua blanket and told him it was his special one for bedtime. *"Did my daddy get this for me?"* I told him I got it and I always will take good care of him. *"My daddy always takes good care of me."* As I laid the blanket over him and said, "I love you, dear little Fruity," he replied, *"I love my daddy."*

Not long after the little guy came, Bob took over his morning routine of eye drops, biscuits and poo time; later in the day he handled dinnertime, more pills and eye drops, and he stood guard while Fruity did his outside business. Like a mother with an infant, Bob hears this fur kid's muted *bwuff* when his bladder is full at some ungodly dark hour, and he gets up to take him outside while I sleep through it all. So Fruity's allegiance to his daddy was understandable and really quite touching.

But not always. When Bob was away for the day and Fruity was back in my hands, he complained that I was late with his dinner. *"My daddy always feeds me on time."* Later I went back in to ask why he was shouting again and he said, *"You forgot my biscuit. Where is my daddy?"* Next he kept wiggling while I was putting drops in his eyes: *"You don't do it right. Tell my daddy to teach you."* And when I asked why he sat in his daddy's lap for hours but he never stayed when I put him in mine, he told me, *"Daddy is soft and you are fast."*

Except for mealtimes and seeking out Bob or me for other kinds of attention, the big dogs entertain themselves by playing in the house or romping around outdoors. I wondered what occupied Fruity's hours while Bob was at the fitness center or doing errands and I was at the computer, and finally I thought to ask what he does when he's alone in his room.

"I see pictures with my inside eyes or hear music with my inside ears."

"That's wonderful! What kind of pictures do you see?"

"Whatever I want. I make them myself and I can make them move like real life if I want to."

"That's wonderful! What kind of music do you hear?"

"Beautiful music! Big Dog said the angels make it. I love that music."

"And I love you!"

"That is a different kind of love."

Even if our dogs come skinny, they don't stay that way, not with extra snacks after Bob and I eat, and when we go out, they expect special treats to make up for our leaving them. The usual biscuits or special dog cookies don't cut it, so, if there are no appetizing leftovers in the refrigerator, we buy hamburgers or chicken nuggets on the way home. Fruity's first special snack was bites of fried chicken. *"This is delicious! I want this every time."* "This is chicken and we don't always have it." *"Did you buy it?"* "Yes." *"Then buy more."*

When he became a bit chubby, I told him he needed more exercise so he wouldn't gain too much weight. Apparently he really took that to heart. One afternoon soon afterwards, I had been especially busy and felt bad about ignoring our little chatterbox, so I took him a biscuit to get rid of my guilt. He told me, *"No thank you. I have to watch my weight."* I needed a computer break anyway, so I sat down beside him and asked what he would like to do.

"I don't know. What are you going to do?"

"Well, I'm really busy and I should get back to work."

"What kind of work?"

"I'm writing."

"Oh. Where is my daddy?"

"He's at a special place doing exercises."

"Does he show people how to do that?"

Bob wasn't a trainer, but since occasionally folks asked him for advice, my reply was a hesitant "Um, yes."

"Now that's *important work."*

Another day when I saw him lying quietly in his room, I went in to stroke him and asked if he was looking at pictures with his inside eyes. *"Not yet."* Had he been listening to music? *"No. I have a lot to do. I am going to be very busy. What are you going to do?"*

"I'm going to write, so I'll be very busy too."

"What do you write?"

"Books and other things for people to read."

"Do they give you money?"

"Yes, when they buy the books."

"Now you can buy more chicken."

Fruity told me he would need a coat when it got cold. I bought him a darling red, white and blue turtleneck sweater that goes over his head and his legs fit through the sleeves. Each day when I was dressing him to go out, he talked about loving his beautiful coat and going out to roam until the afternoon I was rushing and stuffed his head into a sleeve. *"Get me out of this **now**!"*

"This is your beautiful coat, Fruity."

"No it's not. It's a bitch."

"WHAT?! Why did you say that?"

"That is what you say when you don't like something."

So his beautiful coat lost favor, but I ignored his protests that he didn't want it on ever again, and when he darted out of my grasp, I chased him until I won the struggle. His exasperation evaporated as he sauntered as long as he wanted to wherever he wanted to "without the rope." Until the first day it snowed. He walked through the inch or so on the deck, did one poo as soon as he hit the ground, walked around for two seconds to a different spot for two poo, then bolted back up the steps. "Don't you like the snow?" *"Sometimes, but not today."* "Well, the other dogs always like it." *"Maybe they don't know any better."*

The first time Betsy visited after The Little King joined our family, it was only for a few days. Fruity didn't seem to be very impressed with her attentions and disqualified her lap because *"She's quick."* But during her next visit—two weeks of vacation from teaching first grade and a break from university, where she was in the architectural design school—she spent a few hours each day studying in bed and Fruity always wanted to lie beside her.

When I had spoken to him about her during her previous visit, I called her Big Girl, just as I had referred to all other visitors as "Big Girl" or "Big Boy"—it seemed more sensible than rattling off names of everyone who came for only a weekend or so. A day or two after my daughter came this time, Fruity asked, *"Why do you call this Big Girl, Betsy?"* "That's her name." *"Is Betsy a* real *name?"*

And the morning she was packing, he asked, *"What is Betsy doing?"*

"She's getting ready to go back to her home."

"Oh, no! Oh, no!"

"Fruity, she has to go home today."

"Can I go with her?"

"No. She's going in an airplane because she lives far away."

"I can go with her in an airplane."

"Fruity, your home is here with Daddy and me."

"Does Betsy have dogs?"

"Yes, she has dogs."

"She could have one more. I'm little."

"Fruity baby, your home is here with Daddy and me. You can't go with Betsy."

"But I love her!"

The only time I have ever seen him downhearted was after Betsy kissed him and said goodbye.

Unless he is sleeping, he sits up or at least looks at me when I walk into his room, but not this time soon after Betsy left. Even when I gently patted his head, he lay still and kept peering straight ahead. I hoped he wasn't missing her miserably and I asked if he was making pictures with his inside eyes.

"No, this is quiet hour." "What is quiet hour?" *"I think of*

good things and tell God thank you for them. It's what Big Dog told me to do." "Oh, that's a wonderful thing to do! Do the other dogs have quiet hour?" *"I don't know. I don't pay attention to them."*

One afternoon I went into his room with his sweater in hand and touched his head to let him know I was there. He told me, *"This is quiet hour. You never should interrupt quiet hour."* I apologized and made a quick exit. When I went back later, I told him, "You're a beautiful little soul." *"Big Dog said you are too and I have to respect you."* That caught me off guard, and I didn't think until later to ask what respect means to him. *"It means being nice and polite."*

It was Christmas and I told him so. *"What is a Christmas?"*

"It's a very special day for God."

"Then Big Dog must know about it. He always follows God's instructions."

"What kind of instructions?"

"Big Dog tells us what is important to God so we know what to do."

"Didn't Big Dog tell you that Christmas is important to God?"

"I must have missed that lesson. But now I know. Dogs keep on learning like people do."

A few days later he asked, *"Is today a Christmas?"* "No. There's only one Christmas each year." *"What is a year?"* "It's a long time—many, many days." *"Oh. Dogs know what a day is. We don't need to learn about a year."*

Before we left to visit friends one evening, I told him what we were going to do and he said, *"I don't have any friends."* I hugged him and said his daddy and I and the other dogs are his friends. *"I mean a friend who is little like me."* "I don't know any other little dogs." *"Oh, it's all right then."* When I told him our friends had been very sick, he said, *"Tell them I hope they get better."*

The afternoon I walked into my bedroom and was surprised to find Fruity alone on the bed, I asked what he was doing there. *"Nothing. My daddy put me here and I am bored."* Another little bedroom scene was when Bob came into my office to tell me his concerns about Fruity, who was on the bed trembling. I went in and asked, "Are you all right, Fruity? Daddy said you're shaking." He sounded excited when he told me, *"No I'm not, I'm twittering!"*

He had been with us half a year when I said, "I love you" and before I could continue my standard "good night" comments, he interrupted. *"You* always *say that! Why don't you say something important?"* "Fruity, love IS important!" *"I know that, but you* always *say it. Can't you ever talk about something else?"* After that I tried to vary my bedtime remarks, and the time I told him that he is a perfect little dog, he said, *"Sometimes I am a little stinker."*

I really doubt that he knows how often I silently laugh at what he says, but one time after I told him "I love you, Fruity," he said, *"I know you do. It's because I make you laugh."*

One evening nothing seemed to satisfy him. He had gone out to the deck several times, staying only long enough to walk in a little circle outside the doggie door, and he was antsy when Bob or I put him on our bed. Each time we put him down, he walked to his room and yowled until one of us brought him back to our bedroom. Finally I asked him what in the world was he fussing about and he said, *"I am nervous!"*

About that same time his hours in Bob's lap came to an abrupt halt. When I put him there as usual after his dinner and poo outing, he jumped right down. "What's wrong, Fruity?" "*Daddy has pickies.*" It was not a gloating moment—Bob's disappointment was as palpable as Fruity's adamancy that he was through with that lap forever. I thought of all the long evenings ahead for our dear little fellow simply lying on the floor until I had an idea—we would get him a toy and I told him that. "*What is a toy?*" "It's something for you to play with and you will really like it."

Bob and I looked at every toy in the pet store before deciding that the best was a small soft plastic pig that squealed when it was squeezed, and something told me, get a big bag of dried chicken strips too. When I put the pig between Fruity's paws and said, "Here is your new toy," he asked, "*How does it play?*" I picked up his paw, pushed it down on the pig, and it squealed like it was supposed to. So did Fruity squeal—"*I hate it! I hate it!*"—and he ran behind the bed.

The chicken strips were a big hit, though, and each was a new toy every evening for a month or so, until the night I gave him one and said, "Here's your toy, Fruity." "*It is not a toy, it is just food.*" "What?" "*The big one told me.*" He meant Jessie, of course, who was standing beside him, drooling. So I stopped calling chicken strips toys and they remained part of Fruity's evening routine.

Vacuum-gulper Jessie is the only dog who goes into the guestroom—which all visitors understand is *Fruity's* room—and when I give him anything to eat, I take her out and close the door. Bob does the same, and since he was busy in the garage when I heard our little guy barking, I went in to see what he wanted. He was hungry. I prepared his dinner, took it to him and closed the door, but a scant minute later he was barking again. I opened the door, Jessie walked out, the dish was licked clean and Fruity said, *"She ate my dinner."* That girl who will never grow up, who is curious about everything and creates her own fun, who has said nary a word to me and has strategically selective hearing, had been lurking behind the far side of the bed.

One afternoon when Fruity was lying on the bed in his room, I asked if he wanted to roam. *"No, I am busy. I am making pictures of bottles dancing."* "How interesting!" *"They are very pretty bottles. My inside eyes can see their colors."* "Are you making music for them to dance to?" *"No, I can't make music. They make their own music and it is beautiful. It goes chingy, chingy, clinkle, clinkle."*

When Betsy last visited, her younger daughter was on vacation from her first year of medical school, and she came too. I told Fruity that this Big Girl's real name is Raquel.

"Are you sure that is a real name?"

"Oh, yes, definitely Raquel is a real name."

"Well, it isn't a pretty name. She should change it to Ann."

"Fruity dear, she can't change her name."

"I changed mine."

"I know you did, but people don't change their names."

Obviously he wasn't convinced because when I took his dinner to him a little later, he asked, *"Did she change her name to Ann yet?"* "No, and she's not going to." *"Then tell her to change it to Princess."*

A new veterinarian at Monica's hospital said that maybe Fruity's skin condition is exacerbated by food allergies. She suggested that we try a diet of unsalted chicken and rice, and that's what I served him for dinner along with some of the broth. *"This is delicious and it even comes with soup! I love this dinner!"* When I told him he can have it every night, he asked, *"Did you buy a lot of chicken?"* and I told him yes.

"Will the other dogs get some?"

"No, it's all for you."

"That's not fair. Give them some too."

A few evenings ago I gave him quite a bit more broth than usual and he left about three tablespoons. When I picked up his dish, he said, *"You gave me too much soup. I couldn't eat it all."* "That's OK. I know I gave you a lot." Later, when I took him a dessert biscuit, he asked, *"Did you save the soup I couldn't eat?"*

"No, each of the other dogs had a bite. I'll cook more for you."

"You never *bite soup. You* sip *soup. I always sip soup."*

Life with The Little King-Chatterbox is a continuous roll of learning, loving and laughing.

An ever so welcome development came just in time to add it before this story went to press: Fruity is back in Bob's lap and once again the two of them are spending contented hours together.

I told our little fellow how happy his daddy is about this, and as I was wondering what had changed, he said, *"Daddy's pickies are gone."*

"Oh! That's wonderful! What did the pickies look like?"

"You can't see them."

"Then how did you know they were there?"

"I could feel them."

"What did they feel like?"

"They go pinch, pinch, pinch inside and make me nervous."

"But Daddy didn't put any pickies inside you, Fruity!"

"No, I get nervous by myself. I call it pickies, like the briar

that went pinch, pinch, pinch."

"Then why did you tell me that Daddy had pickies?"

"I was with him when I got nervous. I'm not nervous now."

"Oh, I see. It's wonderful that you feel fine again!"

"It's always wonderful to feel fine."

Now *everything* is wonderfully fine again. Whatever pickies are, they have left the building.

Other Dogs

Pusky (poo-ski), a beautiful regal collie, had joined my son Eric's family before Bob and I visited them in Peru. The next time I went alone, after I had learned mind-talk, and Pusky's son Mambo was there by then. The older dog's eyes were dull and he was listless, and soon after I arrived, he told me, "*I hurt. Please tell them*," and Mambo told me, "*He hurts. Tell them.*" The family attributed what I told them to the older dog's aging.

Since my visit was divided between the family's city and beach homes, I didn't see the dogs very often, and the next time Pusky saw me, he told me he hurt and added, "*I'm hungry.*" My daughter-in-law assured me their dogs got plenty to eat. But my last morning in Lima, Pusky came to me and said, "*I hurt. I hurt. Los dientes.*" He must have thought, and rightly so, that pinpointing what hurt—his teeth—and emphasizing it in Spanish would get some action. Eric asked me to walk with the maid to the veterinary clinic, and all along the way Pusky kept telling me, "*Thank you!*"

Not only did the veterinarian understand my kitchen Spanish, but he didn't doubt that I could hear what Pusky told me even before he found that some of the dog's teeth were infected and his gums were raw. As I left the examining room so the doctor could sedate him and then remedy the condition, once again Pusky said, "*Thank you!*"

It was a few years later when I phoned to tell Bob I had finished the errands and would be home in ten minutes. He said Eric had called about Pusky, and it sounded as if he was crying. Bob didn't know if the dog had died or been seriously injured, was very sick or missing. During my drive home, Pusky told me himself.

He remembered that I helped him before and he needed my help again. He was very sick and knew he couldn't get better; please tell the doctor to help him leave. He was concerned about Mambo, who would miss him, and he wanted his family to get Mambo a new companion. Not a puppy, he said. People take care of puppies, but many big dogs don't have homes and life for them was hard. No, he didn't know it was the same for many big dogs where I live, he thought it was only where he was. He talked again about how sick he was, how much he hurt, and please tell his doctor to help him leave. I assured Pusky I would do that and he thanked me.

My son sounded heartbroken when I told him. He said Pusky was at the animal clinic and first thing in the morning, he would go there to carry out the dog's wishes. However, the next afternoon my daughter-in-law wrote that a transfusion had helped Pusky and she had scheduled surgery for him the following day. Her email ended: *I'm going to save this dog!* Of course I couldn't interfere and I told Pusky I was so sorry, but I couldn't do anything more. He said, "*I know. I'll do it.*" Early the next morning the veterinarian called to tell Eric that his dog was bleeding from the mouth and wouldn't survive surgery. The tearful family went to hold their beloved Pusky and say goodbye.

A few days later my granddaughter got a puppy, and grieving Mambo didn't want her. "*She bothers me and I miss*

Pusky." With time and the family's sensitivity to Mambo's loss, he and Blondi became good friends.

*   *   *

Michael and Irmanella, our family in Chile, have belonged to Tanguito for all of his nine years. Having a non-descended testicle instantly stamped him Undesirable in his designer breed that is partly Pekingese, but obviously he doesn't know his caste status because he is the most self-assured, independent, snobbish little guy I've ever met. The meeting was six years ago, and he glared at me for the first three days of my visit. He didn't thaw one bit when I told him he's a great little dog and I'm happy to know him or even when I gave him biscuits. It was only after I told him that I was just visiting, I wasn't going to stay, that he spoke: "*Who are you? Why are you here?*"

Then he went back to his silent treatment. A few days later he and I waited in the car, he in the front seat and I in the back, while Michael went into the Santiago airport to pick up Eric, who occasionally flew in to visit his brother. When Tanguito saw my sons with me and the happiness all around, he left Eric's lap, got onto the console and turned around so he could look at me. "*Now I know who you are. It's all right that you're here.*"

A year ago, when Michael wrote in a panic that a veterinarian had given a grave diagnosis of Tanguito's sickness, intuitively I felt it was wrong and recommended getting a second opinion. "Tuning into" Independence Personified by visualizing him, I told him who I am; did he remember me? Yes, he did. He said he was sick and he wanted rice in chicken broth without any fat in it. Michael wrote back that he didn't know what Tanguito was talking about, he had never had anything like that. Well, Michael, it's what he wants, give it to him.

Two days later I heard from my son again. Tanguito was feeling much better after several small bowls of rice and defatted chicken broth; Irmanella's mother made that for him every time he stayed with her; and the second vet's opinion was far more positive than the first: Tanguito had only an intestinal infection that would be quickly cured with antibiotics and continuing that mild diet.

*   *   *

When I greet dogs who are warming the driver's seat that their human vacated, they look at me suspiciously and if they say anything, it's *"Who are you?"* or *"Why are you talking to me?"* If I were in their place, that would be my response to some stranger who tried to get a conversation going while I'm protecting this car.

Maybe because the beautiful German shepherd in the restaurant was lying at his man's feet made the difference. They were there when we walked in, and after we were settled at a nearby table, in mind-talk I told the dog, "Hello, it's nice to see you here." Without moving a hair, he said, *"I'm working and I can't talk."* The man caught my eye as I was admiring his companion, and he told me about his severe asthmatic condition that the dog could detect prior to an attack. He said his efforts to get Prince to socialize had been futile. When I told the dog that it was OK for him to be friendly with people, he was having none of it: *"No it's not. This is serious work."*

*   *   *

Many other dogs have graced my life throughout the past seven-and-a-half decades. The first was Brownie, who came back as Damian. Skip. Freckles. Snoopy. Charley. Rufus. Critter. Tanker. Cassie. Tango. Ginger. Salty. Bandar. Each has a story, each has a place in my heart.

Dolphins

It was when I was in Peru after the *los dientes* episode and before the end of Pusky's lifetime that the dolphins spoke with me. Several of the family had been able to gather then, and we spent most of those days at Eric's oceanside home. I was pleased when I heard that dolphins were swimming close to shore and delighted that they responded to my thought about that: *"Hello! Yes, we are here."*

I followed my son Michael and another visiting man, surfboards under their arms, to the beach and sat in the sun watching the strong current carry them far down the shoreline. I was thinking that they needed to pay attention to what was happening when I heard, *"Don't worry. We will take care of your boys."*

Half a year earlier, while visiting friends in Puerto Vallarta and celebrating Eric's and Michael's birthdays—my oldest and youngest sons were born six years and two days apart—we went to Dolphin Adventure. As much as I hated thinking of these beautiful souls in captivity, I wanted to touch them and talk to them. While we were waiting our turn in the enormous pool, we walked around the park. A sea lion was sunning beside a tiny, shallow pool, and when I told Bob it was much too small, the sea lion said it was only for him to dive into to cool off, that he had a much larger pool and he likes living there. As I was watching the gorgeous macaws, whose wings had been clipped, one of them told me they didn't mind not being able to fly because they like having people admire them and all the activity.

A film preceded visitors' time in the pool with the dolphins, and we were impressed with the staff's knowledge and diligence in caring for them. Once we were in the water, two people at each corner of the pool, the dolphins took over. The oldest and largest seemed to be moseying around rather than getting with the act, then headed toward me, turned on his side and said, *"We have been waiting for you. Matthew told us you were coming."* I rubbed him gently and told him I felt honored to be there, but I was sorry that he and his friends were not living free in the ocean. He said they don't feel like prisoners and are happy where they are; they're treated well and the excitement of the people in the pool is very good energy for them.

My heart was much lighter about all those animals who are happy in their surroundings, but they are the exceptions to the many that are taken from their families and native habitats and confined somewhere for people's entertainment. It is heartening that there is a growing awareness of our responsibility as stewards of the animals. More and more of us are actively involved in the rescue of domestic and captured wild animals, preservation of native populations, and urging companies to be humane in their raising and killing animals for human consumption.

Mama Deer

Our neighborhood is surrounded by forested hills and the deer who live in these parts safely wander into yards. When we first moved here, they came daily to graze on our back slope, but as our dog family grew, one would spot them and start a chorus of barkers. The deer probably decided there were plenty of other places to go where they didn't have to put up with that noise, and even the special food blocks we put out didn't motivate them to return.

So I was delighted that during summer and autumn 2003, a doe and her young twins came many times. They looked up when I mind-talked: You are beautiful, I love you, you're safe here, our dogs can't reach you, eat all you want. Occasionally one would say *"Who are you?"* or *"Thank you."* The next spring the twins came back. The young buck was braver than his sister, who grazed near the trees while her brother made his way down the slope to eat the buds on the snowball tree near the rock-lined terrace. He and I talked. He knew the dogs were inside the fence. He didn't care if they bark but they frighten his sister. He liked eating the bushes closer to the house. When I asked where his mother was, he said, *"She has new babies. She's taking care of them."*

When he and his sister came the next day, I asked about his mother and the new twins. *"They're too young to come out and she can't leave them."* I told him I would love to see the babies and asked him to tell his mother to please bring them when they are old enough, and during the next couple of weeks, he gave me updates. The day I drove into the driveway and up to the garage, he stood where he was, just a few feet away from the car, and said, *"My mother will bring the babies soon."* I asked him to tell her how happy I will be to see her and the new twins.

Two days later I was at my desk, waiting for the call from Shirley MacLaine's studio. I had followed her film career from "Irma La Douce" and read her books, and I was thrilled that she wanted to interview me and tape it for her Web site. Right after Shirley introduced me and was asking a question, Mama Deer and her babies walked out of the trees into the clearing. The twins, still fragile and brightly spotted, stayed about thirty feet up the slope while their mother walked to the terrace ten feet outside my window and said, *"I brought my babies to show you."*

I could feel Mama Deer's joy and pride in her babies, but I couldn't mind-talk to her and reply to Shirley, who is an excellent interviewer and asks tough questions. I was trying to answer well, but I was feeling Mama Deer's disappointment deepening during the minutes she waited for me to acknowledge her babies, then slowly walk back up the slope and lead them into the trees. My part of the interview was awful—my heart was with Mama Deer and her new twins.

Summertime told me, *"Just tell her you're sorry."* I must have put out that thought a hundred times, but I couldn't shake her feelings or my distress at choosing to ignore her instead of telling Shirley I needed a 20-minute break. If she never called back, that would have been so much easier for me to handle than Mama Deer's heavy emotions that haunt me still.

Three days later the young buck came alone. Even before I saw him, I heard, *"You hurt my mother's feelings,"* and unlike his many previous visits, when even barking dogs didn't deter him from eating his way down to the bushes on the terrace, he stayed at the edge of the trees. I told him to please tell his mother I was so sorry I couldn't talk with her; I wanted to but there was an important telephone call when she came; I'd love to see her and the babies, please tell her to bring them back. As if deer can understand a telephone, but I didn't know how else to explain why I had rejected his mother's gift of bringing her new twins so I could see them.

"I'll tell her, but I don't think she'll ever come back."

She never did. Neither did he nor his sister. The following spring when a doe and buck appeared, I asked if they were Mama Deer's twins. The young buck raised his head and looked at the window. *"She's not my mother, but I know who you mean. We all do. You hurt her feelings."*

Other Animals

Bob made two stylish cedar restaurants, one for birds and the other for squirrels, and hung them on poles a few feet from my office window where I can see the patrons jumping or flying in and out. The squirrels squabble with big jays over the peanuts and even among themselves. If a little one is having lunch, he scurries out when a bigger one jumps in, and if one of the youngsters climbs up the pole when the restaurant is occupied by an elder, the little squirt zooms back down. It's the same with the birds—when a jay flies into the seed dining hall, the smaller birds fly out, and they also give way to the squirrels who decide to lunch on seeds.

When a squirrel wants to tell me something, he (or she) stands on the restaurant roof and looks in the window, and if I ignore that, he hops down to the fence rail. The only thing they ever talk about is peanuts, and like the llama Rainy Day, they say the same things every time. If the nuts are gone: "*There are no peanuts. We have to eat seeds. Tell the man.*" And after Bob replenishes the nuts—we must have the tubbiest squirrels in the world—they say, "*There are peanuts. Tell the man thank you.*"

But one day the sauciest of the bunch said, "*Tell that bird to eat seeds and stop eating our peanuts.*" That was a surprising departure from the standard rhetoric, but even more surprising was hearing from the jay. After saying, "*Tell*

87

him we have to eat too," it picked up a peanut and flew away. I told the squirrel—probably he already knew—and he replied, "*We need to store nuts for winter. We can't store seeds.*"

*   *   *

While our family was driving along back roads in Tuscany, Italy's province that is dotted with enchanting ancient towns perched on hillsides overlooking miles of rolling farmland, we discovered an old manor that had been turned into a hotel for small group meetings. The manager said the next guests weren't due until the following day and we were welcome to come in and look around. Betsy, who is much more sensitive to energy than I, felt the presence of spirits and suggested that I thank them for letting us visit their home.

I did, and a spirit who said he was the son of the builder welcomed us. He was living there by choice, not because he was Earthbound, and his purpose was to preserve the loving energy that had originated long ago and been passed down through many generations. He felt our reverence for his family's home. Most people who came did not feel that, they were interested only in having a good time, and he thanked us for adding to the energy he was safeguarding.

We separated to explore and when Betsy and I met again, she told me to be sure to go all the way up to a turret —the view was fantastic. I climbed the long narrow winding staircase that led to a rectangular opening in the stone wall. My daughter was right, seeing the grounds from that vantage point was not to be missed. That is why I was so slow to notice the little lizard sunning on the slender stone ledge just inches from my hand, and he was looking at me.

I was astonished that he had climbed to that height and hadn't moved when I put my hand so close to him. He told me, *"I didn't move because I know you won't hurt me."* He said "they" knew we were coming, that our light energy had preceded us. If he were in the grass, few would see him, but here he could observe people's close reactions to the kind of life form he had chosen. Even if they didn't find him repulsive, they considered him to be without feelings and intelligence, and he knew I felt differently.

*   *   *

Last summer I was watering the petunias in the flower boxes Bob made for the back fence when I saw what looked like a tiny tan spotted cricket sitting on a leaf. "Cricket" came to mind although I had never seen any like that one, and why had it not jumped away when I started pouring water right beside it?

It started speaking. After it said that what it would be telling me was for the book I would be writing, it embarked on a monologue. At that point this book was no more than a faint idea, but I listened in amazement and all I could say afterwards was that I would not be able to remember anything. The cricket said I wouldn't need to remember, it would tell me again at the right time. I looked up for a moment, then back to the leaf where the cricket had been, and it had vanished.   ....

"Yes, I'm here, just as I said I would be. People have no respect for insects, not recognizing the importance we play in your lives. True, some of us are just a nuisance, like the fleas, but most of us play significant parts in the chain of life that

you feel you're the top of. That's not true regarding intelligence and spiritual knowledge, it's the whales and dolphins that hold that spot, but there's a breadth of intelligence that you call instinct that you cannot even imagine or don't care to bother considering, in the insect life on this planet.

"You don't even notice us unless it's with feelings of repugnance, like cockroaches or ants in your kitchens, and then it's with loathing and steps to exterminate us. I chose to be in this form so I can bring awareness and honor to the insects, who are the most populous life forms on the planet by far. We are interconnected with all other life here, including human, and part of your waking up is acknowledging that we have a part in this drama just as you do. You need to respect us as the interconnected beings we are and respect our lives as we do yours. This is a time when you must choose to rise or fall, and we see that many of you will not rise because you close your eyes to our importance just as you close your eyes to the importance of every human life.

"I think that is enough, Mistress Suzy. I believe I have made my point that humans will fall unless they lift their eyes and their hearts and feel the unity of every life in this world, that every ant and snail has a place in this one consciousness, so does every tree and tiny flower, so does every starving child and every man who has riches. There is no separation. Humans need to start understanding this and acting with respect and honor and help to everyone, every soul life on Earth, and we ALL are souls just as you are.

"Thank you for carrying forth my message. I no longer had need for that body you saw and then you didn't. I made it so you could see me and give me your attention."

*   *   *

Mr. Joe, a large handsome auburn horse, was living in a field near the entrance to our neighborhood when we moved here. If he was in his stable at the top of the hill, he would run down to get the apples and carrots Betsy and her children took him daily when they were visiting. Between those times, treats from me were few and far between. Most of the time I was at home, and when I did go out, I would drive past Mr. Joe and tell myself, Next time do NOT forget his apples.

Now and then I did remember, and as I fed him I always felt sorry that he didn't have a companion. After I could mind-talk, he told me he wasn't lonely, that dogs living nearby came to the fence to see him, children stopped by and said hello, and sometimes people brought him things to eat. From then on I always took something to him when I went out, and often Summertime was with me. While I fed apple quarters or carrots to Mr. Joe, Summertime hung out the window and barked, just a couple of feet from the horse's mouth. Mr. Joe said, "*He's noisy, but he's a nice dog.*"

Eventually the horse started hobbling on his way to the road, and I walked along the fence up the hill to feed him near his stable. He always thanked me for doing that, and one day when Summertime waited for me in the car, Mr. Joe said, "*Tell the dog I'm sorry I can't go down to see him. It's hard for me to walk.*" It was hard for Summertime too, and Mr. Joe outlived him.

Summertime

I wish I could remember what he said that prompted me to ask, "Summertime, are you part of my soul?" *"Of course I am! I thought you knew that."*

That was when I understood why I thought and spoke about him as touching my very soul. Now I understood why my attachment to him was stronger than with any other dog, why my feelings were beyond the love for every dog in my life who has left and every one who is with me now. My bond with Summertime was a shared soul—he knew that all our years together and I knew it only our last month.

That month he was too frail to complete our late afternoon walks, shorter though they were with respect to his weakness. So after we went down the little hill and passed the beaver pond, I carried him back up the hill to our home. He had accepted this gladly until the day before he died. That afternoon when I leaned over to pick him up, he said, *"No. Today I'm going to walk all the way myself."*

Bob and the others continued toward home while Summertime and I zigzagged from one side of the road to the other—it was easier for him than heading straight up. Every few minutes I patted his back and said I would carry him, but each time he told me he wanted to keep on going. It was obvious that he was exhausted. "Summertime, please let me carry you the rest of the way." *"No, I'm going to do this myself."*

When at last we reached the driveway, he stopped and looked up at me: *"Now* that's *success."*

Epilogue

This book was meant only to show the variety and depth of animals' emotions and intelligence. I have just finished reading it all, and there is much more I/me/my than I realized as I was writing. Maybe I am too close to this story for my editor self to kick in, because I couldn't find any places to cut me out and still preserve the animals' personalities and histories or provide the context for what they have told me.

I am thinking back a few years, when one of the clearest psychics I have ever known told me at the end of the reading that someday I would write a book about myself. Until she said that, my reactions to her information had been "Aaah!" or "Hmmm." Now it was "NEVER!" I told her she may be right about everything else, but she is dead wrong about that book. She smiled and said, "I can see it." Since readings are based on what the psychic sees in that moment in an individual's potential future, and because like everyone else, I have free will to choose what I want to do, I knew I never would write anything more about myself.

The four Matthew books reveal more of my life than is comfortable for me. It was the information from Matthew, God and all the other sources that is vital, and in organizing their transmissions for the books, I eliminated my parts wherever possible until I was firmly told to stop that. I was representing the people who also did not understand what

Heaven really is or what the changes going on in our world are leading to, and my questions and comments were the same as many millions of other soul searchers. So in those books, I did what I had been told I must, knowing that never again would I have to put "myself" into print.

It was when I was debating whether to write a little something to wind up this story or let it end with Summertime's triumphant "*Now* that's *success*," that I realized this is the book the psychic saw years ago. Even if there were no I, me or my on any page, the huge part animals play in my life is on every page.

But my purpose in writing about these souls who are so dear to me, and the lizard and cricket with their stunning depth of awareness, is exactly the same as when I typed the first words of the prologue—to show the paramount importance of all animals to humankind because all of us are inseparable parts of God. Animals know this. If *Amusing to Profound—My Conversations with Animals* has inspired you to feel this closeness, then it, too, can declare: Now *that's* success.

II

November 2011

Stories like this don't really end. The storyteller stops, the characters keep on.

When the first part of this book was completed, I felt it met the purpose that inspired me to write it. I didn't think that simply more animal comments could add to our understanding of them and their emotions.

It's what happened during the months after the book went to press that started me thinking, maybe it is important to chronicle this deeper insight into animals' multidimensional awareness and the depth of their love bonds with us.

So I started jotting down some notes—you know, "just in case." The motivation to collect those notes and continue this story came from something that keeps flitting through my head, something Dubby said soon after he joined our family: *"It's all right if I can't see and can't hear well. You love me and love is the best."*

One

It was the end of January 2009, a week or so after the original manuscript was sent to be formatted for printing, when I took Fruity to his doctor and Princess came home with us. Naturally Bob was surprised, but since a precedent had been set with little Lucky, he wasn't shocked because a duo left and two hours later a trio returned, and he welcomed the beautiful young German shepherd whose left foreleg recently had been amputated.

Monica told me Princess' story. Her first family bought her from a breeder of quality stock because they wanted a show dog. But when she was about five months old and her deformed leg and weak hindquarters became obvious, she no longer served their purpose and they took her to be euthanized. Monica would have no part in putting down a healthy young dog, and she told them she would find a good home for Princess.

The first one, with older adults who traveled extensively, didn't work well—Princess's basic needs weren't neglected by the property caretaker, but she had little personal attention. So Monica found another family, where four little children would supply this energetic shepherd with plenty of activity. A few months later the oldest, a seven-year old boy, and Princess were running, tripped each other and her leg was so severely broken that amputation was the only option. The silver lining is that it was her bad leg, which would have been a lifelong problem anyway. Or maybe its deformity is why Princess tripped.

Whatever the cause, it didn't change the facts: Suddenly she had only three legs and her home was back at the hospital because the young mother couldn't handle a baby, a toddler, two other little children and a big, strong, rambunctious dog.

The hospital's largest cage didn't give Princess much room to move about, so one of the vet techs took her home for a few days and brought her back the morning of Fruity's appointment. Even counting her three brief stays at the hospital as one home, Princess lived in six places before she settled in here, when she was one-and-a-half years old.

Despite the emotional insecurity fostered by that nomadic existence and loss of her leg, Princess' Alpha Dog nature was intact. She confidently hopped into the house and let Apple know right away that Boss Dog had arrived. Understandably, their relationship was not warm, but it was doable because neither dog had a fierce temperament and occasional grumbling at each other before going separate ways was the extent of it.

The combination of Princess' insecurity and Alpha Dogness showed itself the first night she was with us. Without invitation or hesitation, she leaped onto Bob's and my bed, shoved in between Fruity and me, put her only foreleg across my chest and asked, *"Are you going to keep me?"* I told her of course we are—this is her home from now on.

"Are you sure? No one else wanted me and I'm not a normal dog. I have only three legs, and I know the other dogs don't like me." Hugging her, I said her daddy and I love her and our other dogs would too as soon as they knew her better. Still, that conversation took place every night for

more than a week before she stopped asking for reassurance.

However, my telling her that Apple, Babe, Jessie and Fruity also would love her was an unmet expectation. Apple wasn't about to befriend a competitive upstart and Babe's tug-of-war games with Jessie ended abruptly because Hot New Player took over.

Babe and Jessie are peers. Their tussles were short and mild, in keeping with older dogs, but young Princess sparked Jessie's Forever Puppyhood. When they weren't at the tugging games, they chased each other throughout the house or outside. Jessie ran, Princess hopped or skidded and fell, but she rose in a flash and resumed the fun. Soon, though, Jessie was ready to quit, Princess wasn't, and much of the time instead of being a playmate, she was a big pest.

If Fruity was in Princess' path as she went bounding around the house, she knocked him over, and when he was enjoying afternoons lying in the yard, she'd push him head over heels, sometimes rolling the little guy over the ledge near his favorite space. With good reason he called her *"that awful dog."*

Nevertheless, the new set of canine dynamics had no serious repercussions until nearly a year after Princess joined our family. Her belligerence toward Babe and his jealousy of her that had been simmering from Day One erupted and even Jessie took part. After separating them and shouting that nothing like that had better ever, *ever* happen again, I asked why they were fighting. Princess spoke first. *"They said you don't love me."*

Of course I hadn't said that or anything remotely similar. I hadn't even *thought* it—I *love* Princess! I asked Babe why he told her something so mean, something he knew wasn't true. *"I didn't say that. She's trying to make trouble."*

Hmmmmm. Since Jessie had been in on the fracas, it didn't seem fair to leave her out of the inquisition even though I knew she wouldn't say anything. Just as she still devoured every paper product foolishly left within her reach, she still hadn't spoken one word all the time she'd been in our family. This is the only dog we've ever had who runs out of the room every time I sneeze, so it was surprising that she stuck around after I'd yelled at her about her disgraceful behavior. Anyway, I asked her what happened.

"He's right, and I didn't say it either."

After hugging this dear old lady until she was nearly breathless and thanking her over and over for speaking to me, I asked Princess why she told me something she knew was wrong.

"They said you don't like me jumping on you and that's the same thing as not loving me."

Oh, good lord! Except for Brillo, who had a ton of street smarts, Princess is the most intelligent dog I've ever known. How could that fine mind so misinterpret plain words? .... Whooooa! She hadn't misinterpreted a damn thing—she was being devious. That's why she got a double lecture: Don't *ever* twist my words like that again! Don't ever, ever, *ever* tell me something that isn't true! Then, for the 100th time, I explained why I tell her NO jumping! I don't like getting knocked down—if this girl had four legs, she could move a grand piano—and it hurts when her nails gouge into my arms and shoulders.

After that hullabaloo, Babe must have decided he was through letting Princess have her own way and he started asserting his right to be beside me instead of deferring to her. But it takes two to tango and Princess didn't want to dance, at least not that night she was lying at my feet while

I was watching the newscast. When she saw Babe walking toward my chair, she leaped up and pushed him all the way back into the hall.

"NO, Princess, *NO!* Why did you do that? Why were you so nasty to Babe?"

"He got into my time zone."

"What?"

"This is my time with you and he butted in."

For all that she may have a "time zone," dogs don't have the same sense of time that we do as far as I've noticed. Maybe how we speak of time has something to do with this, at least according to Fruity when I told him, "Tomorrow I'll take you to get your hair cut."

"When is tomorrow?"

"When you wake up after you sleep tonight."

"When I wake up, it is today."

"Umm, yes, but right now that today is called tomorrow."

"No wonder people get so confused."

Princess is the only dog we've ever had who always looks directly into my eyes when she's talking to me or vice versa. She speaks in complete sentences, sometimes with phrases, and always with an air of authority (that could be air of superiority). And although she has told me many of the same things that the other dogs have talked about, in some cases her perceptions are very different from theirs.

In one of our early conversations, I asked what she does when she goes "there" to visit.

"What do you mean?"

How *weird!* All of the other dogs who have talked with me know exactly what *"there"* is—as well they should, it's *their* designation!—but this super smart girl *doesn't* know?

"I mean, what do you do when you visit the spirit world?"

"I don't visit there, I live there. I have two homes, here and there, and I go back and forth."

I told her that the dogs who left our family before she came to us live there all the time.

"No they don't, not all *the time. Sometimes they're here."*

"What do they look like when they're here?"

"I know you can't see them. Sometimes they look like lights dancing around in the air."

"How do you know what dancing is?"

"I learned it when I watched those pictures and the people said they are dancing."

Bob and I weren't fans of Dancing with the Stars. I had seen it for a minute or two when I walked into the room and that program was on—probably he had been watching something on that channel before he'd left the room. Not that any of that mattered—it was Princess' noticing and remembering that stunned me. I told her she was very observant.

"What does observant mean?"

"It means that you notice things and remember them."

"Oh. Thank you. I'm glad to know another new word."

When I asked her if Big Dog told her we would be her new family, she said no, but she knew from Babe that Big Dog had told him something like that. After telling her exactly how he had come to be with us, I asked if she ever talks with Big Dog.

"Of course I do! All dogs do, and so do you."

"Princess, how do *you* know that?"

"I know what you talk about in your mind. One time you were thanking Big Dog for bringing us together and he told you I'm a very good and intelligent dog because I'm part of a human soul."

And so he had. She isn't part of my soul like Summertime is—that doesn't change just because his body isn't here any longer. What Big Dog told me is that Princess is part of a young soul, and her excitement about life is a reflection of that soul's wonderment and exuberance.

Two

Some would say it was by chance that two months after Princess came, Bob and I were watching the news on a different channel from our usual preference the night a reporter said some of the 27 cocker spaniels the Oregon Humane Society had rescued from a puppy mill already had been adopted. One of those still there must be Summertime's puppy!

Bob wasn't so sure. During our 25 years together, only Jessie had come into our family because I went to a shelter specifically to get her. Nevertheless, the next day we drove an hour to see those spaniels. Except for the two flaxen-haired females who were wagging their tails in cages with their name cards and a HOLD FOR PICK-UP sign, the only one left in that rescued group was a little fellow huddled into a ball at the back corner of his cage. He was wearing a sweater and had been shaved nearly to his skin, but we could see that he was brown and white. Summertime's puppy or not, Bob and I agreed—Dubby needed us.

The Oregon Humane Society is exceptionally conscientious about adoptions. That I'd been one of the first volunteers at our little local HS chapter, even was Dog Chairman (what a title!) for a year, and the Vancouver chapter turned over Jessie to me within a half hour didn't count. The staff of this large chapter wants to meet all family pets to be certain they will welcome their potential siblings and vice versa. So we drove home, packed up Fruity, Apple, Jessie, Babe and Princess and returned. Bob waited with them in the car while I went in and for the first time, could hold Dubby.

The volunteer told me he was ten, had been used as a stud and spent most of his life in a cage. He had cataracts and dry eyes and would need drops twice a day the rest of his life. His teeth and gums were in bad shape and he had hearing loss due to chronic ear infection, but probably his skin condition (that explained the sweater) would clear up. He hadn't barked all the time he'd been there and didn't like being handled.

If we wanted to adopt him, we'd have to come back in a few days—he had to be neutered, needed dental work and more medical treatment for his ears and skin. But of course adoption depended on how the staff felt about this dog fitting into our family.

She said the staff animal communicator, who wasn't there that day, was very helpful in seeing that dogs and adopters are well matched and she would be happy to make an appointment for me. I told her it's wonderful that they have that person on staff, but I didn't think an appointment would be necessary. Maybe she thought it was because during the ten minutes or so I had been holding Dubby, he never stopped trembling.

After the volunteer left to arrange for a meeting room so Bob and our dogs could come inside, I asked him why he was shaking.

"I don't know what's coming next."

I told him that very, very soon he was going to meet our dogs, and if he liked them, we would come back in a few days to take him home, after doctors helped him feel better, and from then on, we would love him and always take care of him. The dear little guy stopped trembling and snuggled his head under my arm.

The staff who rated us thought the meeting of the fur folks went perfectly. They didn't know what Fruity said: *"You told me he's little like me. He's NOT, he's **BIG!** I want a little dog."* Both of them weighed 22 pounds but Dubby has longer legs—still, I'm sure that's not why Fruity peed and pooped on the floor beside him.

Summertime confirmed that Dubby is the puppy he had told me he'd send to us someday. *"I told you he'd look like me but smaller. That's why I called him a puppy, but I knew he would be older."* Then Big Dog chimed in—he wanted to be sure I knew that Summertime had a hand in our finding this little dog who needed a good family. I don't understand how that works, I simply accept that it does. But I couldn't help wondering: If a golden-haired dog like Summertime had been available for adoption, would Bob and I have made a mistake and chosen that dog instead of Dubby?

Four days later we brought him home along with a sack full of assorted pills and bottles of drops for his eyes and ears. The skin infection was clearing up and chocolate brown and snow white fur was growing in. His tiny bit of vision was blurry, and due to extensive damage from many years of infected ears, he couldn't tell where voices were coming from, so he was disoriented and skittish, afraid to light anywhere. When he finally relaxed enough to sit, Princess' maternal genes must have risen to the occasion. Unlike her delight in shoving Fruity around, she lay beside our newest family member and nuzzled his nose.

The Humane Society, or maybe the breeder, billed

Dubby as a purebred cocker spaniel. I think his cocker mother met up with a King Charles gent who happily accommodated her lust. Dubby's head is small, his torso short and chubby, his feet are huge, and his coat grows faster and thicker than cocker fur.

Fruity, who acquiesced to our choosing a BIG dog instead of one his size, asked, *"What is the new dog's name?"*

"Dubby."

"Does he like that name?"

"I think so. It's been his name for a long, long time."

"Ask him if he wants to change it to Ann."

That's when I finally thought to ask why he likes that name. *"Because I love Ann."* Ann was his groomer, a dear woman who treated him gently and talked to him while she bathed and fashioned his fur. Now I understood why he so often asked, *"When can I get my hair cut?"* I should have made the connection when he wanted Raquel to change her name to Ann. If not then, certainly when he asked me my name and he said, *"Suzanne is close so it's all right to keep it."*

I didn't ask Dubby if he wanted us to call him Ann, but I did ask if he likes his name. *"I guess so. Everybody calls me Dubby."*

This little guy wasn't assertive like Fruity, who told me what he wanted his new name to be and why. "If there is a name you like better than Dubby, we could call you that." *"I don't know any other name for me."* I told him Dubby is a beautiful name, it's absolutely perfect for him.

A few days later when we drove him to the ophthalmologist Monica recommended, we took Fruity along in the hope that they would become friends. They knew where we were going and why, and all of us were dreadfully downhearted about the result of the thorough examination: Dubby's cataracts were almost as old as he was and so deeply entrenched that any attempt to remove them could destroy the tiny bit of vision he had and cause nerve damage that would require painkilling medication the rest of his life. The doctor said that cataracts are genetic and he hated to think about all the dogs who had inherited them from our little fellow.

While we were waiting for the written report, Dubby told me, *"I wanted the doctor to fix my eyes so I can see,"* and Fruity said, *"Poor little dog, he can't see. I'm used to it, but he wants to see. Teach him how to make pictures with his inside eyes."* When I related that to Bob, he said he felt like crying. (I already was.)

That evening when I was holding Dubby and told him how sorry I was that the doctor couldn't fix his eyes, he said, *"It's all right if I can't see and can't hear well. You love me and love is the best."*

Despite Fruity's empathy and thoughtfulness, except for sleeping beside Dubby and Princess, who also had become Bob's and my bed partners, he remained a loner among the dogs and seemed more contented than ever to be only with Bob.

Dubby is a mommy's boy. As I move around the house, cleaning or cooking or doing the laundry, he follows me from place to place, probably because he can't see or hear me if he's more than a few feet away. While I'm working at the computer, he snoozes in his basket beside my desk (he loves the basket that Fruity scorned).

Teaching him how to make pictures with his inside eyes didn't work, and the fault lay with the teacher, not the student. Finally I thought to ask Dubby what he sees when he closes his eyes.

"I see whatever I want to."

"So you ARE making pictures with your inside eyes!"

"No I'm not. I remember what I see when I'm there."

After telling him that's wonderful, I'm so happy for him, I asked if he could see me. *"No, but I know you're pretty because I lick your face. You have a nose. I like to lick your nose."*

The HS volunteer was right about "doesn't bark"—Dubby is silent 99.99 percent of the time—but far from "doesn't like being handled," which probably was true enough when his skin was raw, he was starved for affection. The evenings when Bob and I sit in our recliners and watch TV, each of us has a little kid curled up in our laps and the big ones sprawl on the floor around us.

Dubby can't see TV, of course, but even if he could, from what he has said about *"looking at that thing,"* I think he'd be like most of the other dogs who have been in the family through the years—they ignore it. The two exceptions were Summertime, who used to lie as still as a statue and watch intently except whenever an animal appeared—then he'd get up, paw the screen and cry—and if people were fighting, he'd paw at them and bark until the scene changed. More than once Bob or I switched channels because the program was causing Summertime such anguish.

And Fruity, whose deafness and hint of vision still let him enjoy seeing the screen flicker as it changes from light to dark and vice versa. The night that the movie we were watching had an uncommonly dismal background, Fruity jumped off Bob's lap and lay down beside Jessie.

"Fruity, are you all right?"

"Yes, but TV is boring."

Well, not all of these other dogs totally ignore TV. Whenever a phone rings on a program, the big ones bark and run out of the room to see what's happening—even precocious Princess hasn't learned to relate that sound to the picture. Although it was from TV that she learned "dancing," she doesn't watch it—she only glances at the screen from time to time and barks at it whenever she hears animal sounds. Babe and Jessie could care less about those and Dubby can't hear them.

His hearing may be dim and distorted, but he has no problem at all when he's on my lap and I hug him and whisper, "I love you, dear little Dubby."

"I know. That's why I'm happy."

Three

Fruity's appointment with Monica that January day when I met Princess was his second post-op exam after removal of a tumor in his jaw. The diagnosis was the type of cancer that rapidly metastasizes and swiftly is fatal. The prognosis was that he might live two weeks. My friend Ani, a phenomenal energy worker, had started on Fruity immediately, and this day, a week later, Monica was happily surprised that he was healing so well and his overall health had improved.

As much as the little guy liked chicken, rice, hamburger, lasagna and cheese, his absolute favorite food was vanilla ice cream. I hated having to tell him I was really sorry, but ice cream has sugar and sugar makes bad lumps grow and that's why he couldn't have any more ice cream. His solution was, *"Buy ice cream without sugar."* The closest I could come was sugarless frozen vanilla yogurt. He took one tenuous lick, shuddered and yelled, *"I **hate** it!"* and never again asked for his favorite food.

Cancer wasn't finished with our family. Bob started feeling really sick at the end of April, soon after Michael and Irmanella had visited for two wonderful weeks, and several tests and physicians later, we got the diagnosis. Bob had pancreatic cancer.

By then Apple's appetite had seriously dwindled, and although she never complained, it was clear that something wasn't right and the medication wasn't fixing whatever was wrong. It was way past midnight when she nudged me and said, *"I'm very sick and I want to leave. My real mommy is waiting for me."* I told her that in the morning, her doctor would help her go to be with her real mommy.

Ever since Apple had come into our family, she stayed in her nighttime bed near mine until I got up, but when the ringing of the phone wakened me at 7:30, she wasn't there. It was Monica calling. Apple's blood tests showed that she was filled with cancer, like so many other dogs being seen at the hospital, Monica said, and since she had several surgeries scheduled, one of the other vets would come.

After finding Apple lying behind a large rock part way down the front slope, I told her I would dress quickly, then bring her a bowl of water, and a very nice doctor was coming soon. But when I took the water just three or four minutes later, Apple wasn't where I had left her. Teresa came while I was looking in the tall brush and together we scoured the two fenced acres—no Apple.

Not only heartsick about her life with us ending, I also was incapable of thinking clearly. Bob was terribly ill, Fruity's tumor had grown back, and granddaughters who lived in Panama were waiting for me to pick them up at the Portland airport. When Teresa and I walked into the house, there was Apple lying in her foyer bed. She sounded calm, yet excited when she said, *"I've been waiting for you."*

Her last minutes were filled with hugs, loving words and my tears until she peacefully left. After Teresa and I carried her to the van, I wakened Bob to tell him about our dear lady, then left for the airport half-an-hour away. In the seven years that animals and I had been talking, Apple was the first of our fur family who didn't speak to me or send an image after arriving "there." Maybe she did try and couldn't get through to me—telepathic communication doesn't work when someone's practically a basket case.

But I did pull it together so I could drive safely, and on the way, I said "Apple, are you there?" Then I saw her with Juliette. After Apple told me *"Thank you,"* her real mommy thanked me for taking care of her beloved dog for two years and told me she was at peace about her young son. The love bond between them was protecting him from being influenced by the darkness in his father.

Susana and Raquel brought balloons and flowers for their grandpa. They knew about his condition—that's why they had come—but they weren't prepared to see him so weak and ashen yellow from jaundice. Susana gave him her small silver treasure chest filled with smaller treasures, including the wedding band of the ring set her fiancé recently had given her. "Grampy, you HAVE to bring this chest back to me or I can't get married because I won't have my ring!"

She had given Bob an important mission. And he could fulfill it because we were sure he would be in the four percent of pancreatic cancer patients who beat the odds. My certainty wavered the next morning—his body was covered with fiery red splotches. We rushed him to the emergency room, where a team of doctors, nurses and technicians swarmed to stabilize him so a surgical procedure could be performed to treat a whole body infection.

Shortly after Bob came home five days later, Fruity had his turn in a hospital and the tumor was removed again. As soon as I brought him home later that day, he resumed his vigil at Bob's side and told me, *"It's my responsibility to help my daddy get well."* That was the first of many such declarations in the year that followed. Maybe the "pickies" he had felt several months before were the first effects of his tumor. After attributing that uncomfortable sensation to Bob, later he changed his story. Was our dear little fellow feeling the cancer that both of them had then and it was too much for him to handle, but subsequently he undertook the responsibility to help cure his daddy?

Bob's most extensive surgery was mid-July, when his pancreas and spleen were removed and he became an instant diabetic, but there were five more operations to combat infection and two weeks in a rehab center before he came home in September. During that time and afterwards, many of our family came to visit. They were our rock, and in his unique way, so was Fruity.

Every day I told him that the doctors were helping his daddy get well, and if Bob wasn't so heavily sedated that he didn't know I was with him, he loved hearing what our little chatterbox had been telling me.

Fruity spent a few hours every afternoon lying in the front yard. Sometimes when I looked at him through the window, he would be looking around, and occasionally I'd see him move to another spot within the grassy area that was his favored space. One day when I went out to tell him his dinner was ready, he said, *"I'm still with Nature."*

"What is Nature?"

"Nature is God outside."

Another time when I went out to bring him in for dinner, he told me he had just finished quiet hour. "What did you thank God for today?" *"I **told** God something. I told him to make my daddy well **fast**."*

Eventually I thought to ask what he was seeing when he looked around—that's when he started telling me about the fairies. *"They are everywhere outside and they are very happy here."* He said they talk to him when they are resting, and each day he told me more.

"They don't come in the house because they have to work very hard helping the flowers and little plants grow."

"Some fairies are bigger and prettier than others, but all of them are friendly and polite. The smallest fairies are so beautiful. They have shiny colored wings that sparkle and they can fly. They do different work, but it is as important as the big fairies' work."

"The mothers make all the clothes for everyone. They know how to make very good clothes and some clothes are prettier than others. The daddy fairies wear overalls and boots when they work and they wear their pretty clothes for parties. The smallest fairies always have the prettiest clothes."

Fruity said that while the daddies are working, the mothers take care of the children and some mothers teach all the children. When all the work and teaching is finished for the day, the daddies and mothers play games with the children.

Sometimes there are parties and all the fairies come. *"They play games and eat and everyone has a good time. The mothers cook all the food and it is delicious."* (Fruity pronounces it dah-**lisz**-huzz.)

He told me that the mothers love their babies and sometimes they bring them to see him. *"The babies are so sweet and they never cry because their mothers are so good to them."*

Some of the fairies travel far away to help other fairies who have very big jobs, like many plants and flowers to take care of, but they always come home again. *"Sometimes families visit friends far away and the mothers cook lots of delicious food to take to them. They carry it in special little sacks the daddies make."*

One day when I looked through the window, Fruity wasn't anywhere in his circle, and when I went outside, he was nowhere to be seen. I became frantic as my search went on—under the shed, in the briars and other bushes up the hill and down the slope, in and out of the house to see if he had gone in between my stints of looking outdoors. Coyotes roam in this area. Could one have managed to get through the fence?!

It seemed like hours passed before I spotted Fruity lying under a huge fern. As I was hugging him and gasping with relief, I asked if Princess had pushed him all the way down there. *"Oh no, the fairies brought me here! This is their home and it is big and beautiful! I **love** it here!"* The fairies had invited him to stay and he wanted to, but he understood that it's easier for me to serve him dinner in his room.

At last Bob was home! He had lost 40 pounds and was weak, but he was a master at testing his blood sugar, giving himself insulin shots and keeping records of it all for his troop of surgeons and other specialists. As he slowly but steadily was regaining strength, Fruity's tumor was growing back. Monica had told me in January and again in June that it wasn't possible to know if she had removed all the tiny tentacles of malignant tissue, but tests indicated that the disease hadn't spread. Bob and I didn't want our precious little dog to go through that ordeal again, but we didn't want the alternative either.

I talked with Fruity about what he wanted. *"I know the bad lump is here again and I want it out so I can be well. I have to help my daddy get well."* Except during dinnertime in his room or when he had to go out for one poo or both, he sat in his daddy's lap during the day and at night he slept with Bob's arm around him.

He was bouncing back more slowly than the two previous times. Also unlike those days of recovery, this time he refused to eat the baby food dinners. *"It isn't real food and it's terrible."* Sugar or not, that tumor would recur and I wasn't going to deprive him of his favorite food—I told him he could have ice cream again. It wasn't the most opportune time to do that, as I discovered—we didn't have vanilla, but there was strawberry, so without saying a word, that's what I put in his little dish. After he licked it clean, he said, *"This is very, very delicious."*

After that I gave him vanilla or strawberry and he never commented on it. Several weeks later, when I put his dinner on the towel-come-tablecloth, he said, *"I want pink ice cream for dessert."* I'd never mentioned a flavor, much less a color, and asked how he knew some ice cream is pink. *"Big Dog told me there is pink ice cream and white ice cream. This time I want pink, please."*

A few weeks later when I restocked strawberry, I bought caramel swirl too—maybe Fruity would think it also was very delicious. After he ate it, he asked, *"What color is it?"* Since he had color-coded his dessert, I figured that telling him it was white with curvy golden brown lines would just be confusing. I said it was brown. *"Don't buy brown again. Ice cream should never be sticky."*

Four

Bob was feeling good when Betsy, Susana and her fiancé Charlie came at the end of October. At the surprise party neighbors hosted to celebrate Betsy's 50th birthday, everyone remarked about how well Bob looked. We shopped for his wedding attire during the sales in January, and when his brother Roger and his wife Maggie visited later that month, they were amazed at Bob's strength and healthy appearance. By then he had been driving for a few weeks and doing light workouts at the fitness center—partly to get back in shape, partly to once again enjoy the camaraderie of the others in the Old Farts group, as they called themselves.

During those months that Bob was flourishing, Fruity's tumor was growing, and this time it started pushing his eye out of its socket. He said, *"The bad lump bothers me. Get it out because I have to help my daddy get well."* Monica said she could remove it, but the eye would have to go too. *"Tell her to do it. The eye can't see anyway."*

I told him he will hurt a lot afterwards. *"That's all right because then I'll get well."* And when I told him the lump would come back again, he said, *"Then I'll get it out again and get well again so I can help my daddy get well."* A year after the tumor was first removed, Fruity had his fourth operation.

Three weeks later he told me he was well, and along with the others in our fur family, he was left in the care of dog nanny JC when Bob and I flew to Panama with Susana's little silver chest in his carryon bag.

After the 21-hour door-to-door trip, I was worn out but Bob was energized by the excitement of being with our family. The next day we were off to El Valle, a charming little country town in the crater of a long dormant volcano two hours from the city. Susana and Charlie would be married there.

My ex-husband Edmund and my wife-in-law Lourdes, who were at the wedding eve fiesta Betsy hosted for family and guests from other countries, marveled that Bob glowed with good health. He told them happiness does that to folks.

The wedding day was ideal—rain in the morning to cool down the tropical heat and not a drop by mid-afternoon when we left for the church. The ceremony was beautiful and so was the wedding party—Susana was stunning in her lace gown, Charlie was beaming. So was the proud grandpa, who never looked more handsome.

The five o'clock reception was at Lourdes' Tuscany style restaurant, spectacular in its profusion of tropical flowers and roses. We had heard of champagne flowing like water, but that was our first time in the flow. It was our first time at any event as elaborate and vibrant as this.

First Susana danced with Charlie, next with her father and then with Bob. Edmund and I danced, complimenting each other on our fabulous children who had their own fabulous children, and when Bob and I danced, we talked about the family who became his when we married and the love all the way around.

Indoors, banquet tables were kept filled with a variety of cuisines. Outdoors, the band played continuously as guests rumbaed, tangoed, mamboed, salsaed and swayed or bopped, and often laughter was louder than the music. Waiters were constantly on the move replacing empty glasses with full ones and later they meandered through the crowd carrying big bowls of rum punch with long, glowing communal straws. Any germs that went to that reception OD'd on alcohol.

During the night there were three carnavalitos, mini-versions of Latin America's carnaval season with its loopy hats, noisemakers, bulbous noses that light up, oversized sunglasses that blink, garish beads, big plastic neon wigs and other novelties. The third carnavalito ended with a literal bang, a grand fireworks display on the hillside beyond the dance floor. Bob and I were still going strong at 4:00 a.m., when Michael, who would drive us back to Betsy's, said he was ready to call it a night.

Our next adventure was in the Atlantic Ocean. Bob and I rode to the coast with Eric, and what a wild trip it was through the jungle over Panama's continental divide (actually, isthmian divide) and *through* a little river because the old bridge had collapsed and the new one was still being built. We met up with six others who also would spend the next two nights on a tiny island, one of many in the San Blas chain owned by the Kuna Indians.

The two who were waiting at the shore loaded us, our coolers and tote bags in their metal boats with little motors, and throughout the hour ride we were drenched with salt water. We slept in small huts with thatched roofs and dirt floors, ate "catch of the day"—crab, fish and lobster—drank more than we should have, lounged in hammocks, waded or snorkeled and talked about cabbages and kings and things that go bump in the night. We all agreed—it was fantastic!

There were more wonderful days in El Valle and a party

to celebrate Susana's 25th birthday before our flight back home. Bob said those two weeks were the best time of his life.

Five

We knew before we went to Panama that soon after our return Bob would have more surgery, to install a pump in his abdomen to drain fluid into a portable pouch. That was successful and a few days later, he came home.

His constant companion Fruity was becoming frailer and the tumor was growing back, as we knew it would. I told him he didn't have to have another operation, his doctor could help him go there and stay and he would never hurt again. He knew that, he said, but he wanted the bad lump taken out because he had to help his daddy get well. His persistence prevailed and once again, he and I made the trip to his hospital.

The home care nurse and the surgeon felt that Bob's wound was healing slowly but satisfactorily, and he did feel better as the weeks passed. It was after the pump was removed that he started spiraling down—another hospitalization, more surgery, and his grateful return home to hospice care, painkillers and anti-anxiety meds.

From the time Bob got sick, Fruity wakened me for night-time poo, and I was glad in these last weeks that he wanted to chat a bit when he came back in. Strangely perhaps, never were my thoughts about Bob dying, but rather only what I could do for his comfort, convenience and diversion, and he especially enjoyed hearing what his devoted little companion talked about.

Fruity told me he was concerned about the weather because rain every day was hurting the flowers. *"The water stays in the ground and weakens the flowers' tiny roots. The fairies have to work very hard to make the roots strong and keep the flowers alive."* Another time he said, *"The fairies are very disappointed that it rained again, but as soon as the sun comes back, everyone will be happy again."*

The night he stood on the deck several minutes gazing out into the darkness, I asked if he had been looking for the fairies. *"No. I'm looking at the night people who take over when the fairies go to sleep. The night people fly around in the trees and sparkle like stars while they work."* The next night he told me, *"The trees and flowers and the fairies and the night people help each other. They all cooperate."*

The feebler he became, the more often he spoke about profound matters. As I was carrying him back to bed one night, I said, "You are a precious little soul," and he replied, *"I'm a big soul in a little body."* Later, when I told him that he had been telling me more serious things than he used to., he explained, *"As my body gets weaker, so does my brain, and it steps aside and lets my soul speak."*

After each of our middle-of-the-night trips, I'd put him back on the bed with Bob's arm around him and he'd tell me again, *"It's my responsibility to help my daddy get well."*

Then came the night when he didn't say that. He said, *"My daddy is very, very sick. Do you know that?"* I told him yes, I do know. He left Bob's side, walked to the foot of the bed and jumped down—he had never done that before. I put him back on the bed, he jumped down, I picked him up. The third time he jumped, he walked to Bob's chair, lay down and stretched out. I covered him with his blanket and said "I'll always love you, dear little Fruity." He didn't say anything and when I wakened a few hours later, he hadn't moved.

Bob cried when he held him, and reluctantly gave the lifeless little body back to me so I could take our beloved Fruity to the hospital and arrange for his cremation.

I didn't hear from him until that evening, when I asked if he was playing with all our other dogs. He sounded so proud when he told me, *"Oh no, I'm much too busy to play! I'm helping Big Dog!"*

"What? *Already?* Are you with Brillo and Summertime? They're Big Dog's assistants."

After a pause, Fruity sounded more subdued: *"Well, actually, Brillo is training me to be his assistant, but then I really will be helping Big Dog."*

Soon after that, he started talking about his plans to welcome his daddy. What began as *"I'm waiting for my daddy to come"* evolved as the days passed.

"All the dogs will come too. They know my signal."

"We aren't just going to be here when my daddy comes, we're going to have a special reception."

"It won't be just a big reception. We're going to have a staged performance. I planned it and all the dogs know their parts."

"After the performance, we're going to have a big party with food and everything."

Bob laughed as I related each new plan, and the last word on that from Fruity was, *"Everything's ready. We're just waiting for my daddy to come."*

During the two weeks they were waiting, Betsy, Roger and Michael came. All the Old Farts visited, so did other friends and neighbors, and family who couldn't come called or they wrote emails that we read to Bob. July 5, his valiant

15-month battle peacefully ended.

Susana believes that his commitment to taking her ring to her was so strong that he truly did regain his health, and once he had completed his mission, he felt free to move on to a better world. I think she is right.

Nirvana, the proper name of the spirit realm we call heaven, has special entryways for people whose bodies were ravaged by disease, and that's where Matthew and Bob's mother were waiting for him along with the specially trained soul transition team. They all went to the place where Bob would receive customized care to strengthen his etheric body, and Fruity was taken to him.

According to Bob's wishes, his body was cremated. After the celebration of his life for the people here who were closest in his affection, Ani and another especially dear friend helped Betsy and me scatter some of his ashes and some of Fruity's in the same areas where Bob and I had scattered the ashes of our fur family who had gone on before he did. Eventually, when I am ready to leave this home that was our sanctuary, the rest of the ashes will go with the dogs and me to El Valle and become part of the land that Bob and I spoke of as Paradise South.

Fruity let me know that he postponed the reception until his daddy was strong enough. It was about three weeks later when suddenly he popped in and sounded jubilant. *"The performance was perfect! All the dogs were court jokers and my daddy sat on a throne like a king and wore a beautiful robe and a crown like kings wear and afterwards we had a big celebration. We invited lots of other dogs and different animals too, and even some people.* Look!"

He sent me an image of Bob in elegant robes and a jeweled crown sitting on an ornate gold throne, high on a pedestal. The dogs, dressed in jester costumes with ruffled collars and pants cuffs and bobbing hats, were on the stage below. Then the action began, and what a colorful hyperactive bunch! They were twirling around on their back legs, dancing paw-to-paw, doing somersaults and back flips or just jumping all around. They were moving so quickly that I couldn't identify any of them.

Fruity said he'd show me his daddy at the big party. There were so many animals and people in this "film clip" that I couldn't see faces clearly, but it surely was a festive crowd in the midst of floating balloons and confetti. Fruity said his daddy loved it. Later, Bob told me that too, and he described the gala much the way our happy little guy had shown me.

Six

Nothing stays the same. A few years ago the beavers left their large pond and built a dam upstream; last summer the pond was mostly dry land and the creek on this side of the road has become much broader and flows rapidly year-round. Billy Goat died. Two families moved away and I don't know who lives in those homes now. Windstorms have toppled numerous tall firs in the neighborhood and many broken limbs lie at angles against nearby tree trunks. "The fence that Brillo built," which admirably withstood the elements for sixteen years, was replaced by a professionally-constructed five-foot cedar fence.

However, after two years of Bob's several times in one hospital or another, family and friends frequently coming and going, Apple leaving, Bob's and my trip to Panama, Fruity leaving, then Bob, life has been quiet for a while and Jessie, Babe, Princess and Dubby have settled in well. That certainly doesn't mean their actions and reactions never vary, but they're feeling safe and secure in our new family configuration.

My great blessing is that Bob and I can talk about what's going on in our respective worlds. It's natural that we share the same interests as before—our family, human and fur, and our various activities. He is studying, seeing family and old and new friends, playing football and teaching the game to children, attending concerts, and traveling around Nirvana. When Fruity isn't busy training to be Big Dog's helper, he's playing with children and animals, and when day is done, he returns to Bob's apartment in a large complex near a city center.

Their lives are meaningful and fulfilling, and in vastly different ways, so is mine. It's well balanced, with productivity, creativity and good times with friends. I try to make the dogs' lives satisfying too, but except for vet appointments and special good night banter and hugs, they do get short shrift insofar as my undivided attention.

Not long ago I was in my office answering business emails and all of them were sleeping nearby. It was after 4:00 a.m. (I'm a night owl) when Princess wakened, bumped my arm off the keyboard and said, *"Why are you still working?"* I greeted her with hugs—*lots* of hugging goes on here!—and told her it's because there's a lot of work to do. *"You work too much and you're not in balance. Big Dog says everyone needs a balance of work and play. You need to play more."* Big Dog manages some pretty miraculous things, that I knew, but this was the first I'd heard that he teaches puppy souls about the need for a balanced life. Or maybe Princess was being sly, using my respect for Big Dog to produce more play time for her and me.

Somehow it seems more natural now to speak to the dogs aloud, maybe so there's a voice in the house. But that can't be the only reason, especially since I thrive on silence and tranquility, because I also do it when we're walking or are in the car. They always go along on errands—Dubby rides in a padded laundry basket up front with me, Babe jumps into the rear of the '98 Blazer, and the two girls share the back seat.

Even though there is music at home—it's good for the plants—it's what's on the car radio that we talk about. Whereas Fruity could only feel the vibrations (*"It feels jerky"* or *"It's smooth and feels nice"*), Dubby can hear music when he's close to the radio and he uses the same words the other dogs do when I ask if they like what's on. Whether symphonies, concertos or choral groups, their typical opinions (none from Jessie, of course) other than *"yes"* or *"no"* are *it's squeaky, noisy, jumpy* or *OK*.

There have been a few notable exceptions. One day when I asked the group if they like the music, Babe let me know, *"Even if we don't, if you do, we have to hear it."* And then there's his assessment of a Gilbert and Sullivan medley: *"The music is pretty but the people sound silly."* As Dubby and I were on our way to the hospital for his deep ear cleaning, the station's selection was a combination of ancient instruments. "Do you like that, Dubby?" *"I don't think that is music."* The time a lullaby was being played and I asked what they thought of it, Princess said, *"It reminds me of sweet people."* "Who are the sweet people, Princess?" *"They say hello and hug me when they come and they know I'm in charge of the dogs."*

Another of her observations was not that self-centered. After we listened to an especially beautiful piece featuring a violin, she said, *"That's very pretty,"* and I told her it was about love. *"Then that's why it's so pretty. Big Dog said love is energy and it's the best energy in the world."* When I asked my passengers what they thought about another selection that I thought was lovely, Babe said, *"It has melody. Big Dog said music with melody is the best for us."* Without my saying anything about a very lively piece, a short one with drums and cymbals, he offered: *"Big Dog said that kind of music noise is all right a little while."* It seems that Big Dog also gives puppy souls some lessons that relate to the fine arts.

Music is just one of the many topics brought up as I drive. It's almost certain that no other dogs know as much as these kids do about why people go to the post office and the gas station; what school buses' blinking red lights mean; the importance of traffic lights, stop signs and speed limits; vagaries of the weather; what money is and what banks do with it; the things grocery and hardware stores sell; why some trees lose their leaves and others don't; or the variety of food served in restaurants. Those topics always are monologs, though—my captive audience never comments. Maybe it's information overkill and they tune me out.

Most days we go for a walk and I talk to the group along the way, but Babe is the only one who responds. When I told them that walking is good exercise for all of us, he was quick to say, "*Yes it is, but we don't walk everyday because you don't always want to.*"

A new dog on the block raced around her fenced area the second we hit the edge of her property and barked the whole time we sauntered along her road. I told my group, "Probably Big Dog teaches all puppy souls to bark to let people know that they are protecting their property." Babe corrected me. "*No, he doesn't, not all of them. Some are just fancy dogs and when they bark, it means 'I want more attention.'*"

When I asked if they could see any fairies along the road, he said, "*Yes, but they can't play with us. They're too busy working.*" And when I told my group, "Some people say that a dog's best friend is another dog," Babe set me straight: "*We don't like all dogs, just like you don't like all people.*"

The days are gone when Cloudy stopped to drink Earth water and the others followed suit, those days when he and

Brillo and Summertime barked at Rainy Day and Sierra. None of these dogs barks at them. In fact, after a few days of my tossing carrots into the field, Sierra ate from my hand and afterwards, she and Princess rubbed noses through the fence.

Rainy Day always stops a short distance behind his buddy, but still, it's only he who speaks, and whoever would have suspected that my calling them llamas, not lamas, could make a difference in his attitude? It must have had some effect because his first non-derisive comment—a surprisingly long one at that—was: *"These dogs aren't so bad. They don't bark at us. They can't help it if they can't get their own food. You say our name right. Nobody else does. And you bring us carrots. You're a nice woman."*

"How do you know I'm a woman?"

"Because you're not a man. I know the difference."

It's been puzzling why these kids are so mannerly when our walks take us past the llamas' field. Babe solved the mystery the afternoon I thought to ask them, "Did Rainy Day or Sierra tell you not to bark at them?" *"They didn't have to. We know enough not to."*

Now that Princess knows she can plunk herself across my lap (not that very much of her fits), she has stopped jumping on me when I'm upright, and she's the only dog not leashed for our walks. While the rest of us go more or less directly up and down the little hills, stopping wherever ground smells are irresistible, she lopes along at her own pace, falling often or lying down to rest, and meanders back and forth across the road. She feels quite special being the only one with that privilege and I don't tell any of them why she has it: It's tough enough trying to untangle myself from leashes as three kids dart around; no way could I manage four.

Princess' former ho-hum attitude about TV took a U-turn and now she's an avid viewer. Unlike Summertime, who had lain like a statue until he leaped at the screen, Princess responds to whatever noisy action is going on (usually my "me time" is a movie in the wee hours) by bouncing around the room and barking so loudly that I miss the dialogue. Other than this, the innate dignity of her well-bred Self gradually led giddy rambunctious behavior into conduct more befitting her regal breed.

It took a long time of hearing that she's beautiful, intelligent, wonderful, brave and strong; we're family and we take care of each other; we're kind and good to each other; and I love ALL of you dear dogs, before her hostility toward Babe lessened. But much more than my repetitive mantras, it was Babe himself who motivated that change.

All these dogs know that he is our guardian. Princess' breeding dictates that she would serve us well in that position too if she had four legs, but she doesn't and she takes her loss out on Babe. His original reaction to her aggressive-ness—he snarled and snipped back—evolved into silently turning away and even at times rubbing her nose. When I thanked him for being so gentle with her, he told me: "*I know she feels bad about her leg that's gone and I feel sorry for her.*"

Always the gentleman—if you don't take off points for his rare, occasional reproving remarks—Babe is the dog who obeys most willingly, nudges gently for attention, and has "table manners." While the others grab the treats I offer and vacuum their dinner bowls, he delicately takes bites from my hand and dines at a genteel pace. Brillo did that too, but Babe wouldn't even think of using the colorful words that Brillo found so useful to express his displeasure.

Babe can't go as lickety-split as he used to, but he still runs around as if he's trying to round up something or other—his puppy soul's training—but he spends much more time by my side than he did when Bob was here. It could be that since Babe's not as spry as he once was, he's spending more time indoors than he used to, or maybe he's taking to heart what I say to him every night. Along with the litany to Princess, Jessie and Dubby—"We're family" and all the rest—I tell Babe, "You are my forever companion and protector." Then he runs outside and barks to warn whatever is out there in the darkness that the intrepid sentry is on duty and when he comes back, he lies beside my bed.

The history on Jessie's adoption forms includes "very obedient." Either her first daddy had magic words she did respond to or he made up those two on the paper. If I tell her to wait for me, I'll be right back, she's instantly on her feet. If I say "Come now, Jessie," she's instantly deaf. But even at age 12 years, her youthful spirit still glows, and a very recent development really warms my heart—she's *talking!*

There was a long hiatus between her defense against Princess' wily accusation and her next comment, when I gave her one of the bones that had cooled after baking for hours and told her what she had heard on countless occasions: "Jessie, say *thank you.*" That time she said it! But it was many months before she spoke again, a reply to a question I'd asked her hundreds of times: Did she want a biscuit? *"Yes, please."* When I told her how happy I am that she talked to me and please talk more, she said, *"I can't talk. I think."* For six years I had been using the wrong word.

Sometimes Jessie dashes up to me, wagging her whole

body and grinning like a cartoon pup as she announces, "*I'm here!*" The other day she was in her usual place as I was getting the fur family's dinner—underfoot—and I asked if she was hungry. "*Yes. I love dinner.*" "Jessie, do you know Big Dog?" "*Yes. When is my dinner?*" If we never have a serious discussion, that's OK. I'm grateful for the "*thinking,*" however basic it may be, from this dear old lady who often comes around for hugs and licks my cheek when I tell her, "You're Mommy's beautiful girl, wonder woman Jessie."

I thought my days of preparing two doggie dinners were over when Fruity left us. Oh, no. It wasn't long afterwards that Dubby, who for more than a year had relished warmed raw vegetables and meat with kibble for crunch, refused to eat it. "*I don't like it.*" I told him it was the same dinner he had liked all along. "*Now I don't.*" The fourth day he wouldn't even go near his little bowl, I asked what he didn't like about the food. "*I don't like any of it. I don't like vegetables and I don't like hard bites in it.*" If he knew that pulverized flax seeds also are in it, probably he'd have included that too.

Anyway, this hungry little dog practically inhaled a sizable serving of sautéed hamburger mixed into leftover rice. Since breakfast biscuits can scrub his teeth between dental cleanings, he doesn't need the kibble he doesn't want, but the next day I put in a tiny bit of vegetables and gradually increased the amount until he was getting a full complement of yams, carrots, spinach, broccoli and beans along with what he does like. (His catholic tastes in snacks include plums, avocados, apples, mangoes, tomatoes, salad with bleu cheese dressing, roasted garlic, and ice cream no matter what color it is.)

For all that Dubby is the oldest of the family, he seems like the baby. It's partly because when he's not wagging his stubby tail—sometimes the wag goes all the way to his nose—he looks like an adorable stuffed puppy. And partly it's how he speaks, short and simple. Living in a cage for the first ten years of his life gave him little opportunity to hear people talking, and it was the same with his puppy mill mates—none of them had anyone to learn from.

But mostly it's Dubby's dear little self that lets me think of him as a baby. Many times I called him "Mommy's baby" before he said, *"I'm not really a baby. I'm old."* When I told him I call him that because he lets me cuddle him like a baby, he licked my nose and said, *"I cuddle because you make me happy."*

And just thinking about him makes me smile. It isn't that I love him more than the others—love is love is love, and it doesn't come with a measuring stick—it's that he's the sweetest and neediest of the family and I want his life to be as happy as I can make that be so.

The other night I was feeling especially nostalgic, imagining what Bob and I would be saying to each other about the movie that had just ended, a classic filmed in the '40s. I hugged Dubby and asked if he remembers his daddy. *"Not exactly, but I remember I love him."*

Love *is* the best memory, isn't it.

THE MATTHEW BOOKS

Matthew, Tell Me about Heaven
A Firsthand Description of the Afterlife

Matthew Ward
1962-1980

Life in the spirit world we call Heaven is active, vibrant and temporary. Matthew describes the reception of arriving souls, environment, relationships, communication, animals, reunions, nourishment, recreation, education, cultural resources, employment, pre-birth agreements, karma, past-life reviews, and preparation for our next physical lifetime.

Revelations for a New Era
Keys to Restoring Paradise on Earth

Through this book we can learn about our souls, the order of the universe and how thoughts create everything within it, the origin of human life on Earth and human cloning here, and who the reptilians are. Views from Nirvana of our controversial issues show the great difference in the two perspectives, and representatives of civilizations far advanced from ours tell about life in their homelands. September 2001 messages reveal what happened on "9/11" and in the aftermath.

Illuminations for a New Era
Understanding These Turbulent Times

God's descriptions of who He is give us more insight into who we are and the purpose of our multiple lifetimes. To help us understand what is happening in our world, topics of timely importance include Earth's ascension, why there will be no nuclear war, reasons for the invasion of Iraq, how we create our reality, media control, what love is and its power in our lives. More messages from other civilizations and more glimpses of life in Nirvana through Matthew's evolution provide further awareness about past, present and future in our linear time.

Voices of the Universe
Your Voice Affects the Universe: Let It Be with LOVE

The voices of God, Earth souls in spirit, members of our universal family and some of our own show the interconnectedness of All. Synchronicity in life experiences and the influence of the Illuminati give insight into this unprecedented time on our planet as Earth is restored to her Eden self, the Golden Age, and our roles in this transformation.

Order these books at www.matthewbooks.com or your favorite local or on-line bookstore.

MESSAGES

Matthew's messages from December 2003 to date are posted on www.matthewbooks.com. Topics include current events in a universal context, the ongoing spiritual renewal and world transformation, effects of planetary cleansing and Earth's ascension into higher vibrations, and what we can expect during the transitional period through 2012 and beyond, the era of the Golden Age.

Our Family Album

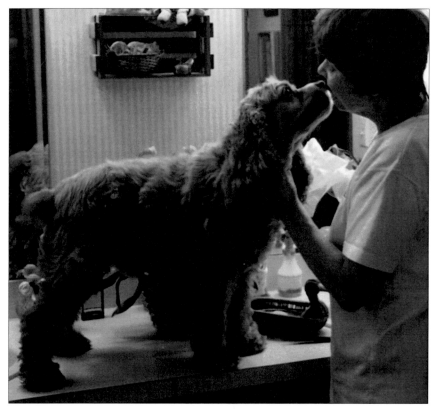

A tender moment with Summertime

My special dear
Sparkle

Summertime
finds a comfy spot

Scrapper — before his name became Summertime —
looks longingly at Molly in her temporary location...
and in her favorite place, the computer keyboard

An older Sparkle sports
her new bandana

Our handsome
gentleman Damian

Courageous
parvo survivor Osa

Brillo, soon after the fence incident that changed his status from "foster" to "family"

Summertime, Cloudy and "the fence that Brillo built"

Cloudy: Midway between looking like a spider and a real dog

... right after digging

... and one morning before digging

Summertime watches Osa getting her new collar

Some TLC for Cloudy after his first leg surgery

Brillo and still-growing Happy on the front deck

Full-grown Happy poses while Summertime inspects a mole hole in the front yard

Bob shows Happy his toy wolf pup

*Brillo eyes his
Christmas present*

Bob snaps Summertime watching me brush my hair

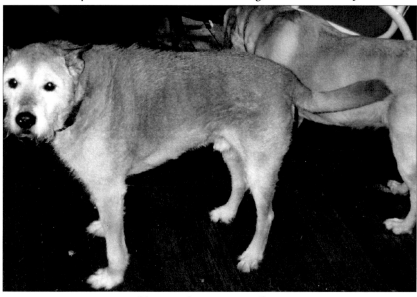

Aging Brillo and perpetual puppy Jessie

Jessie with her loot from the bathroom wastebasket ...

and hoping something good to eat will fall on the floor

Apple surveys her new home
... then solemnly settles in

Chatterbox Fruity on his beautiful blanket

...and in his beautiful coat

*Dear little
soul Lucky*

Jessie is going to join Fruity, who's having a "good roam"

Jessie and Babe playing "tug-of-blanket"

Babe hears Bob calling "Dinnertime!"

Fruity tells me about the pictures he's making with his inside eyes

"My room looks different when I'm on my bed"

"I'm getting old"

Babe loves having Raquel brush him

Apple on "Alpha alert"

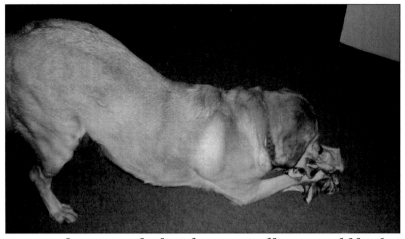

Jessie is devouring the last fragment of her second blanket

Babe's keeping an eye on Bob, who's preparing the fur family's dinner

Sleepy Apple is waiting for her bedtime blanket

Now that the pickies are gone, Fruity is back in his daddy's chair ... here he's waiting for Bob to bring him his evening snack

Welcome to your new home, Princess!

Dubby and Princess expect a snack—why else would I be in the kitchen?

Fruity's nap was interrupted by Princess' pillow-play

"Hey, girl, you better put that back before they see you!"

"My mommy told me to sit here until she gets back"

"Or maybe she said lie down"

Apple's last picture before she left to be with her real mommy

When Bob was in the hospital, Fruity liked to lie in his chair after dinner

Shortly before Fruity's fourth operation ...

... and during recuperation

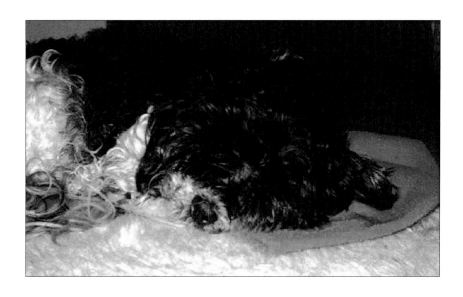

Before guests entered the dance floor, the bride danced with her Grampy

Raquel, Susana and proud mother Betsy

One of the carnavalitos during the wedding reception

Ahhhh, the joys of island-style life!

"I thought I had all of them rounded up—
how did I miss that one?"

Surely Big Dog doesn't teach puppy souls to always be
in underfoot during dinner preparation

Jessie in recovery mode after chasing around the yard with Princess

"Mommy, what is Ani doing?"

Breakfast treats …

… "Thank you, Mommy"

*"I'm not as young as I used to be ...
but I'm still my mommy's forever protector."*

*Dubby
would
rather
snuggle
than
romp in
the yard*

Family